Freud on the Psychology of Ordinary Mental Life

Susan Sugarman

ROWMAN & LITTLEFIELD PUBLISHERS, INC.
Lanham • Boulder • New York • Toronto • Plymouth, UK

Published by Rowman & Littlefield Publishers, Inc.
A wholly owned subsidiary of
The Rowman & Littlefield Publishing Group, Inc.
4501 Forbes Boulevard, Suite 200, Lanham, Maryland 20706
http://www.rowmanlittlefield.com

Estover Road, Plymouth PL6 7PY, United Kingdom

British Library Cataloguing in Publication Information Available

Library of Congress Cataloging-in-Publication Data

Sugarman, Susan.
Freud on the psychology of ordinary mental life / Susan Sugarman.
p. cm.
Includes bibliographical references and index.
ISBN 978-1-4422-0403-4 (cloth : alk. paper) —
ISBN 978-1-4422-0405-8 (electronic)
1. Psychoanalysis. 2. Pleasure principle. 3. Loss (Psychology)
4. Freud, Sigmund, 1856–1939. I. Title.
BF173.S848 2010
150.19'52—dc22 2009053392

™ The paper used in this publication meets the minimum requirements of American National Standard for Information Sciences—Permanence of Paper for Printed Library Materials,
ANSI/NISO Z39.48-1992

Printed in the United States of America

Freud on the Psychology of Ordinary Mental Life

Contents

Foreword

This book grew out of my experience as a developmental psychologist reading Freud. After I began teaching developmental psychology to undergraduates in the 1980s, I recalled the urgings of a college professor of mine to read chapter 7 of Freud's *The Interpretation of Dreams* for the extraordinary psychology of mind it contains. Read it I did and found myself entranced, from the chapter's opening, which describes the luminous and heart-wrenching dream that illustrates Freud's theory of dreams as wish-fulfillments, to the broad theory of mind that occupies the later pages.

In the dream, a devoted father who has just lost his beloved child drifts to sleep in the next room to find himself dreaming the child has arisen, alive, and jostled his arm, saying, "Father, don't you see, I'm burning?" The father awakes to fire emanating from the child's room, where one of the candles lighting the room has fallen on the arm of the dead body and burned it. The father hastens to the room and extinguishes the fire.

Transformative for me at the time was the analytic lens Freud trains on this fragment. He finds it striking that the dream occurred at all when the situation demanded immediate awakening, an observation that, although simple, would probably escape most people; it did me. From this observation Freud extrapolates that the dreamer gained from the dream the opportunity to see his child once more alive and that this desire took precedence over the saving of the few moments he might have gained to spare the body if he had awakened promptly.

Many steps of argument later, Freud makes the case that the striving for pleasure and release from pain drive our entire mental life and that many of its nuances and foibles become coherent in that context. The aforementioned dream serves as a signature demonstration of the claim, because it shows the driving power of the wish, especially in what Freud came to call the unconscious.

In the later argument of the chapter I found myself taken by the discovery that Freud's theory of mind is at bottom a developmental theory. In those pages, Freud was asking what the most minimal condition is from which a mental life could begin that eventually exhibits the complexity and richness of the human mind. As I shall discuss in chapter 2 of this book, he conceives that condition as the discharge of stimuli—in other words, the release from pain—expressed first in the reflex, which expels the tension created by stimuli along a motor path. He then addresses how the "exigencies of life" (Freud, 1900/1965, 604), that is, life experience, necessarily and immediately complicate this simple function.

Striking to me was the agenda of understanding the mind on the basis of its development and the attempt to trace that development to its merest beginnings and reconstruct its complexity from there—while building in the bare minimum of native endowment. For, in addition to the reflex, Freud seemed to stipulate only the capacity to remember.

The great Swiss child psychologist Jean Piaget had proposed a superficially analogous conception of the origin and initial direction of mental development (1936/1952). He, too, conceived the reflex as the point of origin of the mind. We are born, he said, with the capacity to function reflexively and with specific reflexes, such as sucking, grasping, and the eye-blink, already in place. Naturally given to repeat our activity, we but begin to exercise these minimal capabilities and store, or assimilate, the results. Endowed also with the ability to expand our action cycles by the tiniest increments, which proclivity Piaget called accommodation, we begin ever so slowly to elaborate our behaviors. Thus development begins and continues in a self-perpetuating cycle in both behavior and thought.

Although I appreciated Piaget's constructivist idiom and applauded the inventiveness and free-spiritedness it accorded the fledgling mind, I eventually found pervasive logical gaps in the theoretical edifice (Sugarman, 1987). I wondered whether Freud's attempt to account for mental change through the individual's confrontation with a kind of functional necessity might close some of the gaps.

Even though some developmental psychologists eventually contrived solutions of their own to the problem as they defined it (e.g., Greeno, Riley, and Gelman, 1984; see also Fodor, 1972), the field adhered to an agenda that, like Piaget's, described the mind from the outside, based upon ever more exacting observations of behavior. Concepts, reasoning tactics, and other properties of thought were inferred from these behaviors. I count my own empirical research in this group. For a time, I made detailed observations of developmental changes in manipulative play to infer the way in which children might be organizing the materials and their own actions in their minds (e.g., Sugarman, 1983). I was deeply impressed, as I detected Piaget was, by children's resilience and the spontaneous changes their navigation of the world underwent.

But Freud offered something more. He characterized mental life from the inside, from the way it is lived. The way it is lived has to do with what moves it. Thus, for example, whereas both he and Piaget conceived mental life to begin with the reflex, for Piaget the reflex denoted a piece of functional architecture. For Freud it marked the expression of a need, indeed the most fundamental need of humans and other species to rid themselves of pain. The theoretical systems and programs of inquiry they built diverged from there.

Of course, one cannot directly observe how mental life is lived, and psychology is an empirical science. Yet Freud makes extraordinarily deft use of observation in generating his claims, as his canny reading of the grieving father's dream illustrates. He also introduces another type of rigor into his inquiries—a finely honed use of argument by reasoning and example, reminiscent of a philosopher's analytic vise. The enterprise in itself fascinated me. I ultimately found the grounds for some of Freud's claims stronger than the grounds for parallel claims in the ostensibly more empirically driven tracts of modern psychology.

I found myself impressed, finally, by the deep rationalism embedded in Freud's theory. As Freud states in *The Interpretation of Dreams*, those "processes which are described as irrational are not in fact falsifications of normal processes—intellectual errors—but are modes of activity of the psychical apparatus that have been freed from an inhibition" (1900/1965, 644). Even the wildest neurotic symptom answers a purpose. Its premise typically lies hidden, which yields behavior unadapted to the real world and the consequent appearance of irrationality. To explain behavior, and to hold out any hope of alleviating its pain, is to uncover that premise.

I included Freud's chapter from *The Interpretation of Dreams* in my developmental psychology courses for several years and eventually designed entire courses around it and other works. The earliest of the latter courses focused on what I titled "Freud on the Psychological Foundations of the Mind." They elaborated the general theory of mind Freud introduces in *The Interpretation of Dreams* and modified throughout his metapsychological works. But as a student of ordinary, as opposed to aberrant, mental life, I became intrigued all over again when I became acquainted with those occasional works of Freud's that deal with the ordinary.

In these works I again found the developmental analysis, the disciplined argumentation, the rationalism, and the deep feeling for experience that drew me in from the opening pages of chapter 7 of *The Interpretation of Dreams*. My students found them more accessible than they had the more abstract tracts. They lived what was being talked about, and the works, in turn, brought Freud to life. When examined elementally and from the perspective of the exquisitely turned investigatory method that graces their pages, the works prove immensely fertile in suggesting new lines of inquiry. It is that fertility I seek above all to demonstrate.

Acknowledgments

I gratefully acknowledge the support of a grant from Princeton University in the preparation of this work. I thank Ronald Comer for suggesting I write the book and Cindy Hyden for helping me bring it to fruition.

Some material draws from earlier works of mine. Chapter 2 and a portion of chapter 4 draw upon an entry I wrote for the 2008 edition of *The Encyclopedia of the Social Sciences*. Chapter 8 draws upon my *Freud on the Acropolis: Reflections on a Paradoxical Response to the Real* (1998). Chapter 9 borrows from an article that appeared in *The International Journal of Infant Observation* in 2005. I presented a version of the opening discussion in chapter 11 to the American Psychoanalytic Association Winter Meeting in January of 2007.

Part One

THEORY AND METHOD

Chapter One

Introduction to the Inquiry

Walking through pleasing countryside in the summer of 1913 with two acquaintances who could only bemoan the inevitable demise of the scene come winter, Sigmund Freud questioned the pessimistic view that the scene's transience devalued its worth. On the contrary, he suggested to his companions, the limited duration of the vision increased its value and lent it freshness and charm. Impressed by the failure of the suggestion to cheer the others, Freud surmised that a powerful emotional force, which he later identified as the companions' mourning over the anticipated loss of the beauty, interfered with their enjoyment of it. The mind instinctively withdraws from pain and, as it did in this case, disrupts the pleasure it might otherwise gain from its perception.

In the occasional piece "On Transience" (1916/1985), in which he describes this encounter, as well as in his longer essay "Mourning and Melancholia" (1917b/1984), Freud reasons further that, although accepted by the layperson as self-evident, mourning itself poses a conceptual quandary. Given our limited capacity for love, it remains unclear why the relinquishing of lost love objects brings such extraordinary pain, even when replacements exist for the taking. From the point of view of the "economics" of the mind, according to which the mind aims toward the minimization of pain and cultivation of pleasure, we might have been constructed so as to relinquish those objects reality-testing tells us no longer exist, so we might love again. Freud is not exhorting us to feel this way. He is despairing that he cannot align the terrific pain embodied by mourning with the most basic principles of his theory.

It is an enlightening insight that the transience of things could, and indeed does, increase their value. Had the summer scene lasted forever, the two who mourned its ultimate passing might have enjoyed it less than they had the potential to do when aware of its eventual end. One may find oneself equally awakened by Freud's explanation of people's tendency to disparage transience: The disparagement embodies a revolt against mourning. That mourning itself is not self-evident comes as a surprise. It seems only natural that we would rebel against the loss of that which we love. But Freud ends the inquiry there in these early writings, claiming he cannot find the missing explanation. He proposed a solution ten years later in a comment addressed at the end of this book.

Although he is best known for his elucidation of the unusual in human mental life, Freud also attempted to illuminate ordinary human experience, such as people's appreciation of humor, their capacity to become engrossed in fiction, their susceptibility to superstition and religion, and their disposition to a variety of emotional experiences. These last include the uncanny, the stirrings prompted by beauty, and the disparagement of transience just noted. Freud's insights into the everyday and his sense of where within it the productive questions lie reveal an incisiveness that defies both earlier and subsequent thought on his topics.

This book works to expose this version of Freud and to demonstrate its fertility for further inquiry. It reconstructs several of Freud's works on ordinary mental life, tracking his method of inquiry and culminating in a deployment of his tools independently of his analyses. It shows how to read Freud for his insight and generativity and how to push beyond the confines of his analyses in pursuit of new lines of exploration. In this endeavor, in turn, it at once echoes and encourages the spirit of play with ideas so characteristic of, and so engaging in, Freud.

Three features of Freud's investigatory method form the centerpiece of this effort. One is the identification of anomalies of behavior as a means of isolating questions worthy of study. By *anomaly* here is meant less the prima facie unusual than the incongruent in the obvious. Freud scouted out the puzzles that drove the inquiries of interest to this book by looking at behavior with a cultivated naïveté that was quick to spot what didn't quite fit. The incongruity, in its turn, formed the basis not of a portrayal of human mentation as irrational, as Freud is sometimes construed as proposing, but as the point of departure to uncover the logic or, as we shall learn in chapter 3, the "sense" Freud believed lay behind all behavior. The second aspect of Freud's method around which the book turns is the unpacking of the anomalies via an analytic bootstrapping that moves from the testing of simpler and more superficial hypotheses to the construction and examination of more complex and deeper ones. The third feature is the use of the child to understand the adult and the conception of mental development that drives the tactic.

At his best, Freud displayed an argumentative technique whose rigor rivals that of the best of analytic inquiry in other fields. It is my aim to articulate and to emulate this technique—the second focus noted in the previous paragraph—while bringing to light and elaborating the two foci that may be unique to Freud as a means of examining mental life: the identification of behavioral anomalies and the search for the child within the adult.

I note a fourth aspect of Freud's inquiries I shall highlight, if not emphasize. Whether in investigating ordinary or extraordinary behavior, Freud adopted as an early step in his analyses the evocation of the subjective experience at hand. He depicted with remarkable and compelling precision how the experience felt. When attempting to derive an explanation of the experience, he was trying to account for this depiction. This target distinguishes his queries into mental life from myriad others that aim to explain either a behavior described arbitrarily from the external observer's point of view or a theory-derived abstraction.

That is why, for instance, Freud's account of the comic in *Jokes and Their Relation to the Unconscious* (1905/1989) stresses the need for investigation to penetrate beyond the necessary and sufficient conditions of what makes something funny to the question of why laughing is what people do when an event meets those conditions. It accounts for why his passing remarks on beauty in *Civilization and Its Discontents* (1930/1989) exhort theory to reach beyond the delineation of the attributes of beautiful things to an account that explains the feeling that accompanies people's perception of beauty. In his extensive, though scattered, treatment of morality, he labors to account for the compulsiveness of morality and the feelings that accompany moral sensibility, such as moral righteousness and moral indignation, as well as the scope and nature of moral rules.

This emphasis of Freud's on the "stuff" of experiences sometimes resulted in theoretical claims looked at askance by generations of critics who followed him, who have found his recruitment of some concepts odd and uncalled for. Thus, for instance, is his alignment of people's response to beauty with sexual feeling (1930/1989) either dismissed or ignored and his ascription of the development of morality to the resolution of the Oedipal complex disparaged.

But when one feels consumed by the beauty of something or someone, a particular sensation accompanies one's perception and judgment, and any account that purports to give a psychology of the experience of beauty will need to explain this feeling. In speculating that the capacity for this feeling evolved from sexual sensation, Freud was identifying a possible direction for this explanation. He was not reducing the appreciation of beauty to sexual impulse. He was trying to locate an evolutionary source of an experience that seems little connected with the basic needs of humans and yet must be historically linked with them in some way. He was trying to make sense of what otherwise would remain opaque.

Likewise, when we feel we must do something on moral grounds or fear the moral impropriety of a contemplated or completed action—or feel moral outrage at someone else—an intricate set of feelings and judgments comes into play. They involve a mix of compulsion, pride, fear, anger, and sycophantism connected in some way with an identified or unidentified higher authority. With his tracing of morality to the ambivalent internalization of our parents with which we (imperfectly) resolve our Oedipal strivings, Freud was trying to negotiate this obstinately obscure phenomenological thicket.

I note in passing an expository device of which Freud made frequent use in his attempt to flesh out feelings and the anomalies he distinguished more generally: the search for analogies to otherwise puzzling behavior in behavior that is either more transparent or better understood. He applied this tactic most famously in his use of the dreams of normal people as a prototype for understanding psychosis (1917a/1984) and his use of normal grief to understand depression (1917b/1984). We shall see use of the strategy, which Freud generally deployed at the opening stage of an investigation, in several of the works we pursue in the following chapters. We shall see it in, for example, Freud's attempt to unpack the "oceanic feeling" (chapter 5), his attempt to parse the writer's craft (chapter 6), his discourse on the experience of the uncanny (chapter 8), and his attempt to make sense of paradoxical surprise in the face of certainty (chapter 9).

No less a scientist than the eminent neurobiologist and Nobel laureate Eric Kandel has said of psychoanalysis that, even after one hundred years, it remains "the most coherent and intellectually satisfying view of the mind" we have (Kandel, 1999, 505). Psychoanalysis is the study of the mind and psychotherapeutic method created by Sigmund Freud. No other body of thought or research concerned with the mind's workings shows the penetration and systematic sweep of Freud's opus. However, Kandel and even so sympathetic an author as the eloquent psychoanalytic expositor Jonathan Lear believe the potency of Freud's original contribution has been exhausted (Lear, 1998, 32). It is time to broaden the frontier of psychoanalysis, they say, to embrace the directions of inquiry of other fields, such as neurobiology. I aim in this book to show that Freud's original writings remain fertile ground for generative and vigorous investigation into the mind.

I begin with a brief discussion of the portion of Freud's general theory necessary to launch the subsequent inquiries into ordinary mental life: his delineation of the "pleasure principle" and an outline of some of its sequelae. The discussion segues to a sketch of Freud's conception of the development of the mind and a short demonstration of his use of the child to understand the adult. The text proper begins thereafter, with three chapters that track different individual investigations of Freud's and three that branch into new directions.

Chapter Two

The Pleasure Principle

Freud's is a systematic theory, an integrated body of concepts and propositions from which other concepts and propositions follow. It builds from a small group of first principles, elemental parameters of human motivation that admit of no further reduction and yet account for all conceivable instances of human behavior. In this book we shall be concerned with the first such principle Freud distinguished, the pleasure, or pleasure-unpleasure, principle, which he continued to hold dominates behavior even after he introduced modifications to his conception.

According to the pleasure principle, our mental processes always strive to avoid pain and, where possible, attain pleasure. Even behavior that appears inconsistent with this principle as, for instance, the nightmare might appear to do, must in some way align with it. Freud (1900/1965) theorized that nightmares, for example, serve to divert the dreamer from dangerous wishes whose fulfillment would produce frightening consequences. The fearsome content of the nightmare both embodies the dreamer's perception of the danger—such that the dreamer might awake and thereby terminate the dream—and disguises the wish. All dreams fulfill wishes, according to Freud, and in that sense observe the pleasure principle. The wishes fulfilled by nightmares satisfy one part of the psyche, the portion embodying unbridled impulse, which Freud eventually came to call the id, while distressing the portion concerned for our safety, which he later called ego. The nightmare attempts to satisfy both portions, by fulfilling the wish, on the one hand, and representing its dangerous nature, on the other.

In his initial formulation of the pleasure principle, Freud conceived pleasure as a reduction in excitation, or tension, on the model of the reflex. Stimuli impinge on the body's receptors and create a state of tension, or need. Reflexes, such as the eye-blink or knee-jerk, for example, discharge the stimuli, and the discharge relieves the tension. On this model, unpleasure is at bottom a state of tension produced by the accumulation of stimuli, and pleasure is the release of tension resulting from the reduction in stimuli. Although Freud changed his view of the nature of pleasure over the course of his writings, as we shall see later in this chapter, he continued to conceive the thrust toward the discharge of excitation as a primary inclination of mental life.

Thus does Freud surmise that the original and most fundamental function of the mind is the discharge of stimuli, expressed first in the reflex, which releases sensory excitation along a motor path. This simple function must almost instantly complicate, however, Freud infers, because life experience presses the limits of the reflex. Some accretions of stimuli, such as those brought about by somatic needs like hunger, cannot be discharged by reflexive movement. For example, reflexive movements of discomfort from hunger, such as flailing and crying, although aimed to dispel the excitation, cannot remove it. The excitation ends only when the need is satisfied, which, in the case of hunger, occurs through the intervention of the external world.

Lacking any intellectual capability beyond the reflex, the mind at birth has no way to grasp the connection between the movements of discomfort and the arrival of satisfaction. The earliest mind is endowed, however, according to Freud, to form a "mnemic image" (1900/1965, 604) of the perception of satisfaction, after the perception has arisen. This mnemic image attaches to the memory trace of the perception of the need, which has given rise to a mnemic image of its own (p. 604). As a result of this coupling, when babies subsequently experience the need, they also experience an impulse to re-create the image of the perception of satisfaction and the perception itself. Freud calls this impulse a wish. The perception of satisfaction is the fulfillment of the wish.

The shortest path from the perception of a need to its satisfaction would be the evocation of the state of satisfaction immediately upon the experiencing of the excitation produced by the need. The experience of hunger, for example, would immediately prompt the image of the perception of satisfaction. To evoke the state of satisfaction in this way would be to hallucinate, as opposed to satisfying the need in reality. Freud speculates that this shortest path to need satisfaction, the coproduction of the hallucination with the experiencing of the need, is actually traversed in the most primitive mind. Mental life is forced to elaborate when hallucination of the satisfied state fails to eliminate the need, which persists. In a first step toward resolution of this circumstance, babies come to distinguish between the image of satisfaction and real satisfaction.

To achieve this determination the mind must allow itself the perception of the real circumstances that beset it, even if they should prove painful; it can no longer simply sweep away those disagreeable impressions that arise. This switch from the admission of only pleasure to the mind, to the admission of pain so as to allow evaluation of the real circumstances, and ultimately action upon them, represents a major step in mental life, Freud says (1911/1963, 22). He designates the shift in emphasis with a new principle, the "reality" principle, which prompts the mind to determine not only whether an impression is pleasurable, but whether it is real.

The change, Freud thinks, would have provided the impetus to the development of the cognitive-perceptual capabilities necessary for detecting the real, external circumstances and storing the information from these researches: The sense organs, which collect data from the external environment, and the consciousness attached to them would have developed beyond their primordial state, consciousness now sensitive to the qualities of the senses, as well as to the qualities of pain and pleasure. Attention would have developed to give individuals the ability to search the outer world and to monitor the results of their actions there. Memory would have given them the means to notate and store results (Freud, 1911/1963).

Beyond the step of distinguishing real from false satisfaction, the individual would need to form the aim of producing the state of real satisfaction. At this very early stage, the aim of producing real satisfaction would strive toward the reproduction of a state of satisfaction already experienced, as opposed to toward the creation of a state of affairs not yet known. The aim to create this identity, as Freud (1900/1965, 605) calls it, would necessitate the creation of means for achieving the aim, in this case the creation of purposive action. Purposive action arises from the harnessing of motor discharge, which originally served only to unburden the mind of stimuli, for aims remembered in advance (p. 605). Thought, in this series of new acquisitions, could have arisen as a kind of experimental action that would allow individuals to test the (real) consequences of their behavior.

Despite its different emphasis—of assessing the reality, as opposed to the agreeableness, of impressions—the reality principle serves the pleasure principle. To determine the reality of impressions helps one to attain, and guard, one's pleasure in the long term.

Although, Freud (1900/1965) notes, the idea of an organism driven solely by the pleasure principle is a theoretical fiction, because no organism could survive without any reality function at all, the symbiosis between mother and child approximates the function. At the beginning of life, when babies can respond only reflexively and impulsively to accumulating stimuli, which produce the tension of need, the caregiving environment understands the meaning of the discharge and satisfies the need. In this primitive circumstance, babies could, in theory, both hallucinate the fulfillment of the need and have it satisfied in reality. This theoretical possibility helps establish the logical distinction between the impetus toward experiencing pleasure and any mobilization toward the end of resolving the need or, for that matter, any recognition that an end exists to be met.

It has to matter that we begin life with a passive disposition relative to our needs and interests. A desire arises, and we image its satisfaction. Freud conceived as much when he stipulated that our mind runs in two systems: a primary one in which all we do is wish and image our satisfactions, and a secondary one in which we monitor reality and bring to bear there the results we desire. The primary system is the natural one, the one to which we return when stripped of all our developmental and cultural acquisitions, as we are, according to Freud, in our unconscious.

For completeness I elaborate briefly upon a few additional constituents of Freud's system before proceeding with remarks upon the implications of the pleasure principle that bear upon what follows.

Within the compass of the pleasure and reality principles, Freud distinguishes instinct as the driving force of all action. Instinct, as he describes it, is a stimulus to the mind originating within the body that exerts a constant pressure, or impetus, toward relief. More exactly, it is the "psychical representative" of such stimuli, which, on account of their connection with the body, impose a demand upon the mind for work (Freud, 1915a/1984, 118).

But instincts originate within the person and operate at a constant force, as opposed to originating externally and acting at a single impact. Therefore, simple reflexive action, such as the withdrawal of the impacted portion of the body from the encroaching source, has no effect against the impact. One needs to satisfy the instinct. When one's stomach grinds with hunger, for example, one cannot eliminate the discomfort by withdrawing one's stomach from any impinging force. One must eat or be fed. Because instincts require for their discharge machinations more complicated than reflexive action, Freud viewed them as important to the development of the nervous system beyond the reflex.

Freud originally distinguished two classes of instincts, which he believed admit of no further reduction: the sexual instincts and the ego, or self-preservative, instincts. He defined *sexual* broadly to include, with respect to its physical embodiment, excitation to any portion of the body, including the skin, for example, as well as to the oral, anal, and genital areas. Psychologically, the sexual instincts subsume the entire field of erotic relations, including those relations "inhibited" in aim, such as friendships and parent-child relations, which entail positive and even excitatory feelings, but not, in the usual course of conscious life, an aim of genital satisfaction. In their most developed manifestation, the sexual instincts serve reproduction. The ego instincts serve only the individual and have the individual's safety as their object.

In claiming that all human behavior emanates from one or the other of these two classes of instincts, Freud meant that all human impulses and actions remain compatible with one or both fields, not that all human impulses and actions reduce to a sexual or survival drive. One's labors on a mathematics problem reduce to a sexual or survival drive no more than does a sheet of paper to the tree from which the industry milled the paper. Rather, according to Freud, all of our aspirations and behavior must trace in some way to the reflexive bundle from which we arose. The reflexive bundle, in turn, seeks, at bottom, to eliminate the tensions created by its needs and thus to gain pleasure.

Approximately twenty years after he delineated the pleasure principle, Freud (1920/1989) identified behavior he believed violated the principle and attested instead to the operation of a still more primitive force in the mind. In contrast with many other negative experiences that only appear to contradict the pleasure principle, the traumatic, and more specifically war, neuroses, Freud argued, genuinely do so. These neuroses manifest in recurrent dreams, among other symptoms, in which dreamers return to the scene of previous near-death experience and then awake in a shattering fright. For example, soldiers relive attacks in the trenches, and survivors of a train wreck return to the wreck. Each then awakens in a terror that no amount of repetition of the dream lessens.

Although Freud could detect no long- or short-term gain in the cycle, he conceded it could embody an attempt at a purpose. Extrapolating from the observation that the war neuroses tended to afflict individuals who did not incur major injury, Freud surmised that, whereas direct physical insult tends to divert masses of energy to the site of the insult, victims of trauma who escape injury are left with rampant masses of energy released by the shock of the event. Wholly breached, the psychical system attempts to master the onslaught of energy in retrospect, by generating anxiety that, had it arisen during the trauma, would have reduced the shock of the event. But arising as it does after the event, the attempt serves no purpose. The system neither heals nor learns.

Freud extrapolated from these observations to the existence of a tendency more primordial than the pleasure principle and inherent in all organic life: the compulsion to repeat. The tendency can be witnessed in behavior as elementary as the thumb-sucking of human babies or the return of schools of fish to the site of previous spawning, or in behavior as apparently developed as the tendency of human adults to repeat in new relationships the patterns that beset old ones. In the psyche compromised by the war neuroses, the tendency manifested in a mechanical and almost diabolical repetition of a behavior, in total disregard of its impact upon the person.

From his extrapolation to the repetition compulsion, Freud made the admittedly speculative and far-fetched leap to the idea that all living things seek to return not only to previous states, but ultimately to their original state. Given that all living matter began as inorganic substance, all living things seek to return to an inorganic state. They seek to die.

Freud arrived in this way at a new category of instinct, the death instinct, or Thanatos, which he conceived as functioning in opposition to the life instincts, or Eros. After equivocating briefly on the point, Freud subsumed under the life instincts both classes of instinct he had originally defined, the sexual and ego (self-preservative) instincts. Whereas the life instincts, especially as represented by the sexual instincts, seek to unify living matter and create more of it, the death instinct aims to dissolve it.

As Freud originally conceived it, the death instinct denotes the tendency of every living thing to drift toward a state of minimal, and ideally no, excitation. The death instinct of this formulation verges on the pleasure principle, according to which pleasure arises with a reduction in stimulation. Freud soon modified this view, however, in a way that lessened the overlap. Although he continued to hold that the nervous system functions at bottom to rid the organism of tension, and pleasure arises by this means, he acknowledged people's capacity to derive pleasure from an increase in stimulation, as occurs in sexual foreplay, for example. Thereafter, Freud distinguished between the Nirvana principle, which denotes organisms' tendency toward quiescence and hence expresses the death instinct, and the pleasure principle, which encompasses the drive toward pleasure in all its forms, including excitatory ones, and which Freud attributed to the influence of the life instincts (1924/1963, 191).

In the course of Freud's later works, the death instinct assumes increasingly active characteristics and becomes almost synonymous with aggression. Three years after his introduction of the death instinct as the passive drift just described, Freud proposed that individual organisms live long enough to combine with one another, rather than die off, because the death instinct must be neutralized in some way by the life instincts. It is diverted outward over the musculature, he suggested, in the form of aggression, which is eventually directed against others. However, in the wanton destruction he observed in two world wars, Freud perceived an aggressiveness divorced totally from erotic aims and hence a sign of the ascendance of something close to a culture of pure death instinct. He concludes the 1931 edition of his celebrated *Civilization and Its Discontents* with the question of whether Eros would rise again and prevail over humanity.

Chapter Three

Meaning and Determinism and the Search for Anomalies

> The appearance of an incorrect function is explained by the peculiar mutual interference between two or several correct functions.
>
> —S. Freud, *The Psychopathology of Everyday Life* (1901/1989), 354

Many of the remaining portions of Freud's theory follow from the preceding primitives of mental life and particularly from the pleasure and reality principles, which Freud continued to hold dominate mental life even after he developed the idea of the death instinct. One consequence is the idea that all behavior, including the most apparently nonsensical, has a reason, or, as Freud says with respect to psychopathological symptoms in particular, a sense (1917c/1989).

Symptoms, for instance, which might appear bizarre to the observer, represent compromise formations that, on the one hand, satisfy an impulse that has undergone repression (viz., has been pushed from consciousness on account of fear of its content) and, on the other hand, incorporate resistance to the impulse.

Freud demonstrates this etiology in his short introductory work, *Five Lectures on Psychoanalysis* (1909b/1989), with a synopsis of the case of a young woman, Anna O., one of the first patients treated by psychoanalysis, in this case by Freud's mentor, Josef Breuer.

Anna O. suffered from isolated paralyses and an inability to drink, despite unremitting thirst and no organic abnormality that could explain her incapacities. At the time, some enlightened doctors, including Breuer, used hypnosis to try to uncover memories of which patients had no conscious recollection to which such bewildering symptoms might have been responding. Several sessions of hypnosis revealed an association between most of the symptoms and thoughts Anna O. had had while she was nursing her dying father a short time before the symptoms appeared. Her inability to drink dated to an earlier memory.

As a little girl, Anna O. had received care from a governess whom she disliked. Having happened by chance one day upon the governess' dog while it was drinking water from a human cup, Anna felt revolted, but held back her reaction out of propriety. She recalled the scene under hypnosis with a full rush of disgust and despair and awoke pleading for water, after which she had no difficulty drinking. Given that people who feel revolted by something normally find it difficult to eat or drink, Anna O.'s behavior followed coherently from its source; it had a sense. Unlike healthy people who refuse food or drink because they feel revolted, however, Anna O. had no awareness of either her disgust or its source. Therein lay her pathology.

Another class of ostensibly strange productions of the mind Freud believes embodies a sense include parapraxes, or small mistakes of everyday speech and action, such as slips of the tongue. On the surface, the mistakes have either no sense or an unintended one. Thus Freud describes the apparently nonsensical error of a young man who accosted a lady in the street: "If you will permit me, madam, I should like to *begleit-digen* you." Although the word *begleit* derives from *begleiten*, which means "to accompany" and is presumably the term the speaker intended, the apparently nonsensical expression *begleit-digen* mirrors *beleidigen*, which means "to insult." Freud gives an example of an apparently accidental substitution of one recognizable word with another in the remark made by a professor in his first lecture: "I am not *geneigt* [inclined] to describe the services of my most esteemed predecessor." The speaker meant to say, "I am not *geeignet* [qualified] to describe the services" (1901/1989, 94).

Freud suggests that many, if not all, cases of these kinds betray a concealed motive, an impulse seeking expression that is otherwise blocked.

Although one can only speculate about the motives that might produce such errors observed at a distance or reported second hand, one can envision the pathway to the behavior in greater detail when one has access to the mind-set of the actor at the time the presumptive error occurred. Freud opens his landmark treatment of parapraxes, *The Psychopathology of Everyday Life* (1901/1989), with a discussion of his own case of the accidental forgetting of a proper name, that of the Italian Renaissance painter Luca Signorelli, and supplies what he believes to be relevant background detail of this kind.

Although Freud's analysis of this incident may strike readers as arcane, it repays tracking for a glimpse of Freud's masterful argumentation, his meticulous sorting through of data, and his determination of which data could prove relevant.

In the incident, while riding with a stranger toward Herzegovina and discussing travel in Italy, Freud wished to ask his interlocutor whether the interlocutor had seen the famous frescoes in the Orvieto cathedral painted by the Italian Renaissance master Luca Signorelli. Freud could not retrieve Signorelli's name, however, although he knew the name well. Granted the temptation, to be addressed shortly, to attribute such lapses to inattention or chance (1901/1989, 306), Freud believes aspects of the event beg for further explanation. For he not only forgot Signorelli's name, but retrieved two in its place, Botticelli and Boltraffio, also painters. Of those names he knew one, Botticelli, no better than Signorelli and the other, Boltraffio, far less. He wonders, looking back, whether in the generation of the names wrongly remembered he might find an explanation of the forgetting of the name he wanted to recall.

Discerning nothing in the immediate conversation about travel in Italy that would either disturb his recollection of Signorelli or elicit the retrieval of the other two names, Freud reviews the immediately preceding conversation he had had with the stranger, which had addressed customs of the Turks living in *Bo*snia and *Her*zegovina (his italics). In that conversation, Freud had recounted his recently acquired intelligence that that group showed such great confidence in their doctor and complete resignation to fate that if the doctor had to inform them that a loved one was beyond cure, they would reply, "*Herr* [Sir], what is there to be said? If he could be saved, I know you would have saved him" (1901/1989, 11; emphasis in original). The highlighted elements in these references become significant in the chain of associations Freud interpolates between Signorelli and the other names, to be described momentarily.

Freud now speculates that this prior conversation attained the capacity to disturb his efforts in the succeeding one because, as he details next, he had terminated his train of thought in the earlier discussion before completing the train of thought. He had felt a desire to share a second anecdote about the same group of Turks to the effect that they place so high a value on sexual pleasure that they despair irretrievably when afflicted by sexual dysfunction and claim to find life no longer worth living; the perspective juxtaposes oddly, Freud notes, with the same people's resigned attitude toward death. Freud paraphrases a patient as having told his doctor with reference to sexual dysfunction, "*Herr*, you must know that if *that* comes to an end, then life is of no value" (1901/1989, 12, emphasis in original). Freud suppressed his desire to relate this material in his conversation, he says, out of propriety in talking with a stranger. He speculates that he also may have blocked the evocation of a further, related recollection, the news that had reached him while he was staying shortly before at the hamlet of Trafoi in the Italian Alps: A patient of his with an incurable sexual disorder had taken his own life. Although, Freud insists, he did not engage this memory consciously during his ride to Herzegovina, the phonological overlap between *Trafoi* and the incorrectly retrieved *Boltraffio* leads him to suspect the memory, and his resistance to it, were activated in him unconsciously during his conversation with the stranger.

The availability of a motive to suppress a content—the painful memory of the news at Trafoi—and the evidence, in the form of the acoustic associations between the suppressed content and the names that surfaced—Boltraffio, Botticelli—convince Freud that his forgetting of the name *Signorelli* was motivated, rather than accidental. His verging on the reference to Signorelli aroused toward consciousness a content he wanted to forget, and his aim to forget became realized on another content. As Freud frames the circumstance, he willed himself to forget one thing, but forgot another against his will (1901/1989, 13). The substitute names he brought to consciousness, *Botticelli* and *Boltraffio*, instead followed the pattern of compromise in symptom-formation in psychopathology. These two names, which may initially strike the observer merely as arbitrary selections from the network of names of painters Freud knew, retain fragments of both what Freud wanted to forget—Trafoi, associated by acoustic similarity—and what he wanted to remember: Signorelli, associated by both acoustic similarity and conceptual connection (all three were Italian Renaissance painters).

Freud admits as curious the idea that he might have been attempting to forget one thing (the patient who committed suicide) and forgot something else instead, or in addition (Signorelli's name) (1901/1989, 13). He suggests that this displacement occurred by means of the repressed material drawing the wanted name (Signorelli) into the repression via an associative connection—between the *Herr* of the anecdote that led Freud into the chain of associations leading toward the death of the patient with the sexual disorder and the *Signor* of Signorelli (p. 14).

A more straightforward result of the will to forget would be to forget the undesired item (Freud, 1901/1989, 13). But the frequent result of repression is precisely to disturb mental process. It would be consistent with that kind of disturbance if

Freud's suppression of the migration of his thoughts toward the news at Trafoi distracted him from the task at hand, which was to retrieve the name of the painter of the frescos at Orvieto. One could add to the impact of that suppression the possibly diverting effect of his conscious decision—for other reasons, namely, propriety—to withhold from his conversation the anecdote that came to mind from which the Trafoi associations would have followed. Although conscious, Freud's withholding of the second anecdote, about sexuality, represented a choked intention, which, Freud leaves the implication, would itself come at a cost.

Students encountering Freud's analysis for the first time find themselves bewildered by its apparent arbitrariness. It would seem simpler to assume *Signorelli* lacked sufficient salience in Freud's mind for him to access it easily. One would expect the turn of the conversation to travel in Italy to train anyone's attention more on the sights one might see, in this case the frescos in the Orvieto cathedral, than on the names of their creators. That *Signorelli* existed in Freud's mind in a network of related names would have made it all the easier for Freud to generate alternatives to the missing name. Modern accounts of what is also known as the tip-of-the-tongue phenomenon—the sudden failure to remember familiar contents of memory—proceed along these lines (e.g., Schacter, 2001).[1]

Freud also admits the possible operation of this more straightforward type of mechanism, "*simple cases where proper names are forgotten*," as opposed to "*a type of forgetting which is motivated by repression*" (1901/1989, 17; emphasis in original). However, he found the occurrence of such behavior improbable. Although some mistakes, such as slips of the tongue, might occur when people operate under fatigue or other stresses, the mistakes cannot be caused by these limitations, he believed, because other similar mistakes occur when people remain fully attentive (1909b/1989, 29). Further, precisely because numerous associative pathways lie open and can cause a person accidentally to utter one word instead of another (in the case of slips of the tongue), one needs to explain why a given pathway is chosen on a given occasion.

His reservations about the simpler mechanism aside, Freud is more interestingly read on the stronger view, toward which he veers by the end of *The Psychopathology of Everyday Life* (1901/1989, 307), that there are no accidents in mental life. All mental happenings, like our mental endowment in general, come from somewhere, and the first clue as to where lies in the striving of mental processes toward the attainment of pleasure or relief from pain.

From this vantage point, Freud's account can be seen to explain why, when he failed to retrieve *Signorelli*, he generated *Botticelli* and *Boltraffio* instead of the myriad other names of Italian painters he presumably knew. They bore an acoustic resemblance to *Bosnia*, the setting of the topic of the previous conversation. It also explains why Freud's thoughts might have begun to travel back to the sad news he received at Trafoi. The sentence from the preceding conversation, "Herr, what is there to be said? If he could be saved, I know you would have saved him," resembled the sentence from the anecdote, which he withheld, of which this story reminded him: "Herr, you must know that if *that* [viz., sexual function] comes to an end then life is of no value." The latter, withheld story affords a direct, substantive connection to the suicide of the patient who had suffered an incurable sexual disorder.

The account so far falls within the realm of the straightforward associative processes that contemporary psychology, and Freud, would ascribe to the routine workings of thought and memory. What Freud adds is the idea that his ultimate failure of memory, in retrieving the name *Signorelli*, had a motive. Given the easily plausible eventual drift of his thoughts toward his patient's suicide, he extrapolates that his mind would have wanted to block this trajectory. We learn from his account that he had worked extensively with the patient. The loss of the patient via suicide must have signaled a defeat for Freud and possibly, to his mind, a tragic failure of responsibility on his part.

Perceived self-depravity can form an especially potent trigger for repression, as Freud describes in his account of another patient, Elisabeth von R. This patient succumbed to hysteria after entertaining and suppressing the thought, while mourning her recently deceased sister, that she now might have the opportunity to marry the sister's husband (Freud 1909b/1989, 22–23). This dynamic lends credibility to Freud's claim regarding the Signorelli incident that, had his thoughts begun to travel toward his patient's suicide, he might have attempted to inhibit the flow.

But, as is more drastically evident in the case of Elisabeth von R., who developed a full-fledged neurosis, repression engenders sequelae. Accordingly, Freud posits two consequences of his supposed repression of thoughts about his patient who committed suicide. One is the derailment of his attempt to recall a different content (Signorelli, the painter of the frescos at Orvieto), which Freud claims became tied to the unwanted material via an associative connection (between the *Herr* of the anecdote Freud surmises began the chain of thoughts leading toward the patient and the *Signor* of Signorelli) (1901/1989, 14). The other is the production of extraneous content, the names *Boltraffio* and *Botticelli*, which occurred as Freud searched his memory for the name of the painter of the Orvieto frescos. Bol*traffio* nonetheless gave voice to the unwanted memory. Suppressed elements, Freud says, exert pressure to assert themselves elsewhere (p. 15), and the availability of associative connections facilitates the process.

It remains to incorporate the delayed action of the repression into the account. The chain of associations leading toward the lost patient presumably unfolded during the conversation that preceded the one in which Freud tried, and failed, to retrieve *Signorelli*. Freud attributes this delayed action to his having terminated the previous line of thought before it reached completion. He had withheld from the conversation the anecdote about the Bosnian Turks' response to the loss of sexual function and then, in turn, presumably repressed the associations to his patient that might have followed from the anecdote. It is not difficult to imagine that choked intentions might remain active.

Perhaps the weakest link in Freud's explanatory chain is the idea that his attempt to forget the matter of the suicide would have invaded his attempt to retrieve the name *Signorelli*, via the overlap between *Herr* (from the anecdotes leading to the unwanted thoughts) and the *Signor* of Signorelli. By contrast, both the line of thought leading to the suicide and the attempt to block the line come across as plausible happenings. Although one can conjure up the image of the pool of thoughts concentrated upon *Herr* getting in the way of *Signor*elli, given the equivalence of *Herr* and *Signor*, the connection seems remote. Freud builds a more convincing case for the intrusion of unwanted thoughts in his accounts of slips of the tongue and even, in the case of this instance, of his retrieval of the less familiar *Boltraffio* via the association with Trafoi.

It is tempting to imagine simpler mechanisms, like a more general distraction of mental function occasioned by the attempted repression, and perhaps by the withholding of the second, "delicate" (1901/1989, 12) anecdote about the Bosnian Turks' attitudes toward sexuality, from which the unwanted line of thought presumably followed. Given that proper names are more liable than other words to evade memory, *Signorelli* could have eluded Freud's grasp.

It is not clear how much greater plausibility this alternative account has than Freud's does. Freud's analysis holds the advantage that it explains why *this particular retrieval* might have proved difficult at the moment. It also makes use of the evidence Freud plausibly sees—via his generation of *Boltraffio* and the easy association between the anecdote he withheld from his companion about the Turks' sexual attitudes and the matter of the suicide—that the suppressed anecdote and the suicide were active in his mind.

Especially clear in Freud's analysis of this incident is his commitment to the existence of a psychical explanation for the merest nuance of thought (from Strachey, 1965; cited in Freud, 1901/1989, 8). The explanation derives ultimately from the effort of mental processes to relieve themselves of pressure, that is, the pleasure principle (see chapter 2). Given the minute detail into which Freud's explanations descend, they give the appearance of extreme arbitrariness. How does one know that *Signorelli* slipped from Freud's conscious grasp because it got sucked into a realm of thought he was endeavoring to avoid? How does one know that it vanished through an attraction exercised by the phoneme *Her*, found in the words *Herz*egovina and *Herr* that purportedly evoked and ultimately ignited his retreat from the content he wished to avoid? One does not know.

But when one adopts the stance that *something* must determine even the tiniest wrinkles of mental life, that purely chance events are highly improbable and perhaps inconceivable, then the resulting pathway to behavior will be complex. If one accepts the idea that thought moves largely associatively, then the pathway will boast interconnections. This is the scenario Freud's analysis depicts, with the insertion that the process in this particular case became influenced by troubling material he endeavored to avoid that, as per his more general model, would inherently seek expression.

To assume that all behavior has a sense is to ascribe to it a payoff, the very object of the pleasure principle, which holds that all mental activity, granting Freud's exceptions, strives for the relief of pain and the cultivation of pleasure. Within this desideratum lies the essence of Freud's conception of the psychological explanation of a behavior. To explain a behavior, one needs to locate its payoff to the individual. Thus, to explain a symptom or a parapraxis, either of which might appear counterproductive or even painful to the individual on a superficial reading, is to identify the impulse or impulses it might satisfy. To explain or "interpret" a dream is, as we observed at the beginning of chapter 2 with respect to the nightmare, is to recover the positive, wish-fulfilling function or functions its different elements might be serving.

In the extract from Freud's essay "On Transience" (1916/1985) with which this book opens, one can again see how the pleasure principle guides Freud's search for an explanation of a behavior. He notes as curious his companions' despondency in the face of the beauty surrounding them that, given the dictates of the pleasure principle, ought to have brought them only pleasure. In a situation that ought to bring pleasure, why would one feel unhappy? Something in the situation, he reasons, must be provoking pain instead of the expected pleasure. The anticipated loss of the beauty brought his companions pain, he concludes based upon their comments, and, consistent with the pleasure principle, the mind naturally withdraws from pain and thus in this case disrupted the pleasure it might otherwise have enjoyed.

This pattern of argument appears repeatedly in Freud's writings. A behavior appears to contradict the pleasure principle, thus inviting exploration. On analysis, the behavior can be shown to conform to the principle. The way in which it does so affords a psychological explanation of it, or at least the beginning of an explanation.

The pattern of argument extends beyond the scouting for apparent exceptions to the pleasure principle to anomalies more broadly, as is already highlighted by Freud's treatment of the so-called parapraxes. Here stand behaviors that defy logic and meaning, and not only and not even necessarily our striving for pleasure. Later—for example, in Freud's account of his apparent "disturbance of memory" on the Acropolis—we shall see that it is sometimes sheer paradox, as opposed to an evident violation of the pleasure principle, that alerts him to the possible existence of quirks of mental life whose investigation might expose previously unplumbed laws of the psyche. In those as well as other cases, however, the pleasure principle soon emerges as the anchor point of the analysis that subsequently unfolds.

NOTE

1. As demonstrated by modern experimental psychology, names prove especially prone to forgetting because, by comparison with

ordinary words, they lack a conceptual connection to their referents. In one experiment research participants were told that some among a group of people in photos had the last name *Baker* and some *Potter*. Those participants were less able to recall the correct match between photo and name than were different participants who learned that some people in the photos were bakers and some potters. People's occupations convey more about the people—for example, when they get up, what they wear, what they do—than do their names, which have only an arbitrary connection to them. Researchers believe the absence of conceptual connection leaves names more prone than common words to weakening in memory (Schacter, 2001, 63–69).

Chapter Four

Conscious and Unconscious, Repression, and Development

Freud's signature delineation of a field of "unconscious" mentation also flows from his idea that people operate under the pleasure principle and that this type of operation dominates early childhood. He believed one could not explain human behavior without the assumption of a series of mental events that occur outside awareness (1915b/1984). Only once one interpolates mental acts that occur outside one's notice can one make sense of both superficially incoherent behavior—such as dreams, symptoms, and parapraxes—and numerous everyday behaviors, such as ideas that emerge suddenly in our thought.

The separation between conscious and unconscious mental processes arises, according to Freud, primarily through the operation of repression, a reflexive and hence infantile response driven by the pleasure principle. In repression individuals withdraw consciousness from painful or frightening impulses in the manner in which one might withdraw one's hand from a hot stove. The pain can be caused either by the impulse in itself or the individual's anticipation of the external consequences of acting upon the impulse. The repressed impulse remains in unconscious memory, sustained by its struggle for expression and simultaneously denied that end by the interests that originally led to its repression.

In the final chapter of his *Totem and Taboo* (1913/1989), Freud postulates a second, smaller category of inherited, as opposed to acquired, unconscious ideas. This category includes the most primitive embodiments of the instincts and impulses that, based upon an analysis of modern emotion, he concluded must have been passed along by earlier generations. The latter impulses include guilt for the killing of the primal father and a portion of the hostility that led to the presumed deed. In the just-mentioned analysis of modern emotion, Freud concludes that the extremes of emotion displayed by small children outweigh the eliciting circumstance to such a degree that they must draw upon an extraneous source. They outweigh the eliciting circumstance, according to Freud, even taking into account children's intellectual immaturity and consequent lack of perspective and the myriad mental dynamics resulting from early relationships.

Important implications follow from the existence of repression for the development of the mind. Insofar as the mind becomes a repository for repressed impulses and impressions, behavior becomes determined increasingly by sources one cannot detect. Or, to depict the trend from the perspective of the observer, human behavior follows a developmental trend from more transparent to more complexly derived and thus more obscure. Whereas, Freud (1900/1965) observes, for example, the dreams of small children often express the unfulfilled (conscious) wishes of the previous day, adults' dreams contain bizarre and inscrutable imagery; one must painstakingly unpack the imagery to uncover its instigating dream thoughts. Although the motives of children's sense of humor are clear, as seen for instance in their sense of superiority over a clown, adults, who may laugh from similar motives, do not know what they are laughing at (Freud, 1905/1989; see chapter 7 of this book).

Trends of these kinds arise, Freud believes, from both the separation of conscious and unconscious thought, which makes repression possible, and the natural "surmounting" of one developmental stage by another, as Freud calls it in "The Uncanny" (1919/1885; see chapter 8 of this book). Regarding the latter process, when one stage succeeds another in development, both the mode of experience embodied by the earlier stage and the experiences accrued in it remain in the psyche. They continue to exert an influence there, though reshaped by the superimposition of later stages.

In one of the most lyrical passages in the psychological literature, which appears in the opening pages of his *Civilization and Its Discontents* (1930/1989), Freud entertains different models for the manner in which earlier and later stages might coexist in the mind.

The configuration might, for instance, resemble that of the city of Rome, in which remains of former incarnations of the city lie in layers beneath the modern metropolis, some remains still visible above ground, though mostly much decayed. The mind, Freud says, shares with this image a copious past in which remains of earlier epochs continue to exist beside recent developments.

But in the mind, he imagines upon reconsideration, earlier epochs continue to exist fully realized, whereas only traces remain of the earlier epochs of Rome. Similarly, drawing upon a different analogy, Freud notes that although one can identify in the body of an adult animal or human the outline of the child's bones, organs, and tissue, the original is absorbed into the later version. The embryo does not exist in the adult. In the mind, earlier developmental structures persist (1930/1989, 16–20).

The result of the interaction of mental stages Freud perceives is behavior that, on the one hand, bears the imprint of childish ways of being and, on the other hand, exceeds these traits. Therein lies the pivot around which Freud's investigations of human behavior turn.

Chapter Five

Developmental Analysis as Investigatory Tool

> The idea . . . sounds so strange and fits so badly with the fabric of our psychology that one is justified in attempting to discover a psychoanalytic—*that is a genetic*—explanation of such a feeling.
>
> S. Freud, *Civilization and Its Discontents* (1930/1989, 12, my emphasis)

In his attempt to unpack and explain adult behavior, Freud looked for the child within the adult. All of our behavior traces ultimately to its origins in childhood, and some of our otherwise inscrutable behavior bears this mark especially strongly.

In the instance captured in the epigraph, Freud was attempting to understand the "oceanic feeling," a term coined by the French novelist Romain Rolland in reference to the impression, experienced by some people during bouts of religious ecstasy, that they are at one with the world. Rolland had suggested to Freud that the basis of people's susceptibility to religion lay in this feeling. While conceding that people might experience the feeling, Freud found Rolland's account of it dubious. Freud could infer no basis upon which people might receive a direct "intimation of their connection [to] the world" through a feeling directed expressly to the purpose (1930/1989, 12). Such a connection is not a tangible physical reality. Moreover, it runs counter to our normal adult sensibility, which observes a clear boundary between self and world. Thus, he turned to childhood to attempt to identify a source from which the experience might flow more coherently.

Preparatory to doing so, Freud attempts an amplification of the experience through a comparison of it with a feeling he surmises to be similar, for which he can offer a conveniently concrete embodiment. He cites in this connection the sentiment of dramatist Christian Dietrich Grabbe's *Hannibal* when Hannibal faces self-inflicted death: "We cannot fall out of this world" (1930/1989, 11). It is the sense of "nothing can happen to me" that Freud hears in the impression of an indissoluble bond with the world and for which he now seeks a possible developmental source.

Babies and children have a less clear boundary than adults do between self and world. Nursing infants do not distinguish an external source as the origin of the sensations flowing to them (1930/1989, 13). They gradually make this distinction on the basis of their experience. For example, some sources of excitation, which we know to be babies' organs, can provide sensation at any time, whereas others, for instance what we know to be the mother's breast, appear only when screamed for (p. 14). Babies find, correspondingly, that they can withdraw from some sources of pain, for instance, contact with what the observer knows to be an external object, and not from others, such as hunger, which comes from within (p. 14; also Freud, 1915a/1984, 114–17). Experiences of this kind prompt a distinction between inner and outer, though not necessarily at the correct boundaries initially.

Freud speculates that adults' capacity for the oceanic feeling might draw upon the earliest sensations of unboundedness. The sensation, moreover, coincides with a period in life when we enjoy total dependence upon our caregivers, from whose protection we progressively detach as we grow older. Religion, Freud offers, answers the universal human desire to return to this dependent state. The oceanic feeling evokes the sating of the desire and thus derives from the source that drives religion, rather than constituting that source.

Freud seems all but unique in the methodological strategy of using the child to understand the adult. The discipline of developmental psychology, which formed mostly after him, proceeds primarily in the opposite direction. It uses the adult as a template for examining the child. It identifies idealized adult "end-states" and characterizes children's abilities by their degree of approximation to that standard. It does so often to the neglect of what is childlike about children and how they progress from that state to adulthood (Sugarman, 2005). There is much to be gained in adopting Freud's strategy, both in the understanding of adult behavior and in the identification of fruitful lines of inquiry with children, as the following chapters attempt to show.

If, as Freud's discussion of the oceanic feeling suggests, one can gain insight into adult behavior by extracting its childlike voice, one may find at times that this method fails to produce complete illumination. The childlike voice identified, something in the behavior remains unaccounted for. The adult and child versions of what is ostensibly the same thing do not align completely. Freud recognized this potential clearly and used it for further leverage on the investigation of the behavior. As detailed earlier in this chapter, his view of the adult incorporates not only the adult's origins in childhood, but also the myriad layers of development that follow and interact with the primitive base. It follows, then, that to understand some adult behavior, one must tease apart the contribution of the child and the contribution of this additional dynamic. Some of Freud's most intriguing investigations of ordinary mental life follow this template. I take up three, in turn, in the chapters that follow, each highlighting, in addition to this investigatory pattern, additional methodological tactics or interestingly different perspectives on mental development.

Part Two

STUDIES

Chapter Six

Getting Lost in Someone Else's Story: "Creative Writers and Daydreaming" (1908)

Even the parapraxes of mental life discussed in chapter 3, such as slips of the tongue or the momentary forgetting of known names and words, consist in aberrations of mental function, as do more flagrant departures from normalcy such as neurotic symptoms and dreams. They thus form natural points of departure for investigation. One wants to know by what means the mind we know as performing otherwise can produce these results. In the realm of what I have called ordinary mental life, or our usual everyday doings, no such question arises. Things just go along; we do what we do. Nothing cries out for explanation, because what goes on is the usual, ordinary, and obvious.

In his inquiries into ordinary mental life, rather than hold up the self-evidently extraordinary for investigation, Freud found the curious in the obvious and interrogated *it*. Thus, in launching his pursuit of the question of by what means creative writers manage to capture and then engross the casual reader, Freud identified a puzzle. Everyone knows the experience of becoming riveted by a book: becoming drawn in by the plot, invested in the characters, and mesmerized to the point that one needs to wrest oneself forcibly from reading. From a detached perspective, it is not clear why this should happen. The characters are nothing to us, they are neither relatives nor friends, and they are not real. Why should we care what happens to them? What is the hook?

Not even the writers best able to induce in us the narcosis of pleasure reading can tell us how they make on us the impression they do, says Freud in his 1908 "Creative Writers and Daydreaming." Freud focuses his inquiry initially around the sources from which the writer's craft springs. In this discussion I center on the reader—the receiver—and the process that enables the reader's response. The reader's process forms the part of the puzzle that concerns ordinary mental life and comes increasingly to dominate Freud's essay. The processes of writer and reader remain deeply interconnected, in any event, as Freud conceives them.

Freud's essay dwells upon the so-called B novel: works, in his words, "not [of] the writers most highly esteemed by the critics, but [of] the less pretentious authors of novels, romances, and short stories, who nevertheless have the widest and most eager circle of readers" (1908/1985, 137). These are the works that put us in a trance, the proverbial page-turners we cannot put down. Freud addresses the question of what is happening in this reaction and from what piece of human psychology it proceeds.

Freud begins his investigation with the search for an endeavor of ordinary people that resembles the writer's craft, which he, and writers themselves, find so elusive. He identifies imaginative activity as that endeavor and next traces its developmental origins, which he finds in children's play. Both children at play and creative writers fashion their own world according to their fancy. They take this world seriously, investing it with great emotion, and at the same time distinguish it from reality. Some languages, Freud notes, preserve the connection between children's play, which utilizes material objects of the real world, and creative writing designed for tangible presentation in the theater. For example, one says *play* in English and *Spiel* in German; *spiel* appears in the terms *Lustspiel* and *Trauerspiel* ("comedy" and "tragedy," respectively).

As people grow older, Freud says, they exchange playing for daydreaming, in which they continue to invent worlds molded to their fancy and fueled by their emotions. They abandon only the connection of their fantasying to tangible objects. However, whereas children happily expose their play to onlookers, adults conceal their fantasies. Freud attributes the disparity to the difference between the wishes that drive children's play and adults' fantasies. Children's play realizes the wish to be big and grown up, a wish they have no reason to hide. Adults' daydreams fulfill unsatisfied erotic and ambitious wishes, which they would feel ashamed to expose. Freud gives as an example of a typical adult daydream the fantasies of a man on his way to inquire about a job. The man imagines getting the job, impressing his employer, becoming indispensable in the firm, being taken into the employer's family, marrying his daughter, and eventually taking over the business. The series reproduces, according to Freud, the protecting house, loving parents, and first love objects of childhood, all projected into an adult vision of the future through the use of the material of the present.

Freud identifies the same ingredients in the B novel: a hero who manages to survive and triumph despite adversity, whose success is sufficiently guaranteed that one reads along in security, and whose invulnerability exposes the blunt egotism of the story. In addition, the desirable women in the story fall in love with the hero, thus completing the erotic side of the fantasy. Freud believes that although many creative pieces depart significantly from this "model of the naïve daydream," one can link even major deviations to the template through intermediate cases (1908/1985, 138).[1]

Freud claims creative writers draw upon their own wishful fantasies in constructing these stories. A contemporary experience, he says, awakens the memory of a childhood experience, and the evocation generates a wish that finds embodiment in the creative work. By contrast with the daydreams of ordinary nonwriters, which would evoke only disinterest, the creative piece entices the reader with carefully woven disguises and purely formal aspects of narrative construction that remain the writer's gift. Thus captivated initially by what Freud views as the incentive bonus of the text, which he likens to the foreplay of sexual intercourse, readers go on to achieve deepest pleasure from the release of preexisting tensions in their minds. The tensions consist of erotic and ambitious wishes now able to find fulfillment.

To become riveted by a text is to have one's attention thoroughly focused on the world emerging from the pages and one's emotions flowing within that world. Freud's account of the forces that enable this absorption aims at the heart of this reaction. The reaction, he says, is tantamount to daydreaming, indeed *is* daydreaming, and is sustained by the mechanisms that sustain a daydream. The effect begins with "tensions in our minds" (Freud, 1908/1985, 141), which express our most basic wishes. Unlikely ever to satisfy these wishes fully in real life, we seek their fulfillment through fantasy. When we find ourselves gripped by a story, the writer supplies the fantasy, which releases our own fantasies.

Aside from whether the effect of pleasure reading actually does arise via the mechanisms Freud details, Freud manages with this account to evoke the experience. In peak daydream, one forgets the passage of time and one's surroundings. One glides along effortlessly, absorbed, entertained, and gratified. And one can emerge from the B novel, as one can from the daydream, feeling "had," guilty, perhaps, for having let some side of one other than one's elevated, respectable, industrious self take over.

Although he may have begun with an analogy to arrive at this alignment, Freud ends up with much more than an analogy. He makes a case for how the experience of pleasure reading came to be what it is and, in doing so, evokes the sense of the experience all the more strongly.

NOTE

1. Freud accounts for the pleasurable effects of stories and drama with distressing content somewhat differently (see, e.g., "Psychopathic Characters on the Stage" [1906/1985]).

Chapter Seven

Why We Laugh at Something Funny: *Jokes and Their Relation to the Unconscious* (1905)

In the analysis of the "oceanic feeling" (chapter 5), the child provided the pathway to understanding an adult experience. In the analysis of pleasure reading, discussed in the last chapter, the search for analogs in childhood illuminated the adult experience part way. The analysis then exposed a divergence between child and adult that, in turn, provided leverage on the adult experience. Freud's treatment of jokes and the comic posits a still more intricate interplay between child and adult acquisitions as the basis of the adult capacity.

Jokes and Their Relation to the Unconscious (1905/1989) shows Freud at his analytic sharpest. This work, one of Freud's longest, contains a systematic dissection of a phenomenon in which the process of inquiry holds at least as much interest as its outcome.

Focused around jokes in particular and eventually the comic more generally, the work raises the dual questions: When we laugh at a joke or comic display we find incredibly funny, what are we laughing at, and why is it laughing that we do? The answer to the first question is less straightforward than it might appear and provides an axis of contrast between child and adult. The latter question comes to the heart of the human capacity for humor.

Because they compose a rich and well-defined set, jokes admit of progressive, step-by-step analysis and thus afford a portal to process and mechanism that might prove more elusive with the study of the broader and perhaps more intuitively appealing class of the comic in general. In anticipating the reader's potential disinclination toward the narrower topic, Freud points out the "intimate connection among all mental happenings" and the consequent potential illumination of other areas by discoveries in even one confined domain (1905/1989, 13).

Reviewing the scant literature of his time on jokes, Freud remarks upon the disjointed nature of the accounts on offer, which otherwise strike him as individually apt, if insufficiently general. The accounts single out, for instance, a judgment that produces a comic contrast, bewilderment followed by sudden illumination, a playful judgment, play with ideas, sense in nonsense, brevity beyond what the content would normally admit, and similarity in the dissimilar. One wants to know how these determinants might interrelate, for example, what bearing the brevity of jokes might have upon their playfulness or whether a joke must satisfy all the characteristics so far defined. Freud thus aims for a more unified treatment than this list affords, beginning from a classification of the material itself. He will draw the classification from the existing literature and from fresh examples that have struck him as especially funny, in other words as clear cases.

Especially in translation, many examples may fail to move the modern reader. That reader can still appreciate the drift of Freud's argument and the astuteness of his observations, however. Even where the individual jokes fail to captivate, one can easily track the comparative assessments Freud makes of different offerings. It is the comparisons, and not the valuation of individual samples, around which the analysis turns.

The ninety-page second chapter of Freud's book, entitled "The Technique of Jokes," undertakes to determine whether it is the thought or the expression that turns a remark into a joke. By rephrasing sample jokes into other words, which he calls the method of "reduction," Freud demonstrates that the expression, or joking envelope, produces the joking effect. Thus, he rephrases the joke, "I drove with him *tête-à-bête*," as "I drove with X tête-à-tête, and X is a stupid ass" and easily shows that the latter remark scarcely raises a laugh (1905/1989, 25, emphasis in the original). The reduction in hand, he can characterize the maneuvers by which the remark is turned into a joke. By use of the overlapping sounds in *tête* and *bête*, the joke "condenses" the two terms into one. The condensation, moreover, takes place within the frame afforded by the conventional *tête-à-tête* and thus eliminates any direct reference to *il est un bête* ("he is a stupid ass"). The replacement of the *t* in the second *tête* with the *b* of *bête* now serves as the sole representative of the omitted reference. Freud terms the entire process "condensation accompanied by slight modification" and suggests that the slighter the modification the more satisfying the joke (p. 25).

In proceeding to "reduce" a long litany of cases in this fashion, Freud gradually expands the list of apparent joke techniques, which includes, in addition to condensation, the multiple use of the same material and double meaning, for example. The multiple use of the same material can be seen in *Traduttore—Traditore!* ("translators are traitors") (1905/1989, 36) and the double entendre in the courtier's reply when asked by Louis XV to make a joke of which the king might be the subject (*sujet*): *Le roi n'est pas sujet* ("The king is not a subject") (p. 40).

Some jokes move beyond a simple play upon words to a play upon logic, as is seen in bath jokes like the following: When two men meet near the bathhouse, one asks the other, "Have you taken a bath?" The other replies, "What? Is there one missing?" (1905/1989, 55). Although the joke engages the double meaning of the word *taken*, it also diverts the train of thought to a different track via a shift in psychical emphasis from "Have you taken a *bath*?" to the implied question "Have you *taken* a bath?" (p. 58, emphasis in the original). In this diversion it accomplishes a deeper one, from the implicit reproach in "When is the last time you took a bath?" to a reprimand of the questioner: "What an idiotic question!"

The following bit of sophistry, which drops the play upon words altogether, operates similarly: A tutor in a small town who took to drink eventually lost most of his pupils when his vice became known. A friend dispatched to prevail upon him to change his ways exhorted him that he could get the best tutoring in town if he gave up drinking. The indignant miscreant protested, "I do tutoring so I can drink. Am I to give up drinking so I can get tutoring?" (Freud, 1905/1989, 59). Although it engages no play upon words, even this example depends upon its form, specifically in the rearrangement of the same material, here the means-ends relationship between drinking and tutoring. Freud shows this dependency via a reduction of the tutor's retort into the conceptually equivalent: "What a senseless suggestion [to give up drinking to get tutoring]! The important thing for me is the drinking, not the tutoring. After all, tutoring is only a means to enable me to go on drinking" (pp. 59–60). The joke disappears with this translation.

Paralleling his effort with verbal jokes, Freud proceeds to tease out, test, and codify the techniques that appear to operate in conceptual jokes. He also examines the sufficiency of the techniques in accounting for the presence of a joke and determines that many joking forms appear in non-joking venues as well. Although some jokes depend upon representation by allusion (1905/1989, 94) and analogy (p. 96), for example, these forms also appear in earnest discourse. Other conditions must be met, therefore, for them to yield a joke.

Freud ends this first phase of his analysis at this juncture absent a complete delineation of the conditions sufficient to produce a joke. He believes he has sampled the domain of joke techniques broadly enough to have extracted the most common and most essential varieties. These, he contends, all converge on an economization of some sort, the connection between economization and pleasure to be investigated later. He finds the survey complete enough to justify another later comparison between the techniques of joke work and the mechanisms of dream formation. That comparison will license the stipulation of the interplay of unconscious processes in the production of jokes.

Having pursued the analysis of joke technique in isolation as far as he thinks he can, Freud begins to approach the joke process from other angles, starting with an examination of the purposes of jokes. He perceives these to fall into two categories, which cross the division into verbal and conceptual jokes and thus make use of either array of techniques. Tendentious jokes carry a potentially offensive message, of a hostile, obscene, cynical, or skeptical nature, according to Freud's further classification. An example of a hostile joke would be "To be sure, the man was not a great light [*Licht*], but a great candlestick [*Leuchter*]. . . . He was a Professor of Philosophy" (1905/1989, 98). Innocent jokes carry no intent beyond the word or idea play that composes them, as in "One person procreates a thought, a second carries it to be baptized, a third begets children by it, a fourth visits in on its deathbed, and a fifth buries it" (p. 108). They represent joking in its purest form, granted Freud's subsequent caveat that the distinction is somewhat relative, and jokes thoroughly innocent of any ulterior purpose may remain the province solely of childhood (p. 162).

Freud insists that innocent jokes, however, like tendentious ones, serve at least the purpose of evoking pleasure in their audience and confer it upon their teller. For the aim of all joking, and perhaps of aesthetic ideation in general, is to draw pleasure from mental processes (1905/1989, 113–14). Indeed, Freud takes the opportunity to suggest, we probably do not undertake anything without some intention in view. If we do not need at the moment to dedicate our mind to the relief of an essential need, then we let it work in the direction of pleasure, which includes its drawing pleasure from its own activity (p. 113).

Tendentious jokes nonetheless tend to elicit more intense pleasure than do innocent ones, Freud observes. He infers on this basis that they draw upon sources of pleasure unavailable to innocent jokes. By means once more of his method of reduction, he shows tendentious jokes manage to impart content whose direct expression would encounter obstacles. Thus, the humorist Herr N. remarked of a praiseworthy, but flawed gentleman, "Yes, vanity is one of his four Achilles heels" (1905/1989, p. 26),[1] implying, but not saying, that the gentleman was an ass. Whereas the hero Achilles had but two heels, of which one was vulnerable, only an ass has four heels.[2] Harking back again to basic principle, Freud traces the added pleasure of tendentious jokes to the disarming of a repression. Repression generally turns something formerly agreeable, in the case of the Achilles-heel joke the direct expression of hostility, into something aversive. Renunciations of any pleasure tax the psyche, which is all too eager to find a means of release of the impeded impulse.

If the pleasure of jokes comes from both their technique and their purpose, the question arises of how pleasure arises from these sources and, further, whether a unified account might not explain both.

One can see the mechanisms by which pleasure is generated more easily in tendentious than in innocent jokes: People achieve a satisfaction they could not attain otherwise. The joke allows them either to lift an existing inhibition or avoid constructing a new one to meet an external obstacle that has arisen. The first would arise when propriety dictates there are some kinds of things one does not say, and the latter when one wants to deliver an insult whose direct expression might lead to negative repercussions from an external party. Both the maintaining and erecting of psychical inhibitions require what Freud describes as an expenditure of psychical energy. It takes work to inhibit the flow of mental activity in the direction in which it wants to go. If an inhibition can be made unnecessary, then the energy that would have been expended upon it is saved. If, therefore, a joke allows the lifting of an existing inhibition or the avoidance of the construction of a new one, then it enables a saving of energy. It thus embodies an economization not only on expression but more broadly on psychical expenditure in general.

Given the absence of tendentious content in innocent jokes, the pleasure induced by these jokes must derive from their techniques, Freud surmises, and he makes the case that that pleasure, too, traces to a savings in psychical expenditure. To this end, he divides joking techniques into three groups, each of which enables this savings in a different way.

In the first group, sound receives emphasis over meaning, such that the hearer is transported fluidly from one circle of ideas to another not normally connected with the first. Freud cites the following example: At the end of a meal at which the host served a *roulard* (or *roulade*), known for its labor-intensive preparation, a guest asked whether the delicacy had been made in the house. The host replied, "Yes, indeed. A home-*roulard*" (1905/1989, 112; emphasis in the original). The joke associates the kitchen and politics merely via a commonality of sound (between *rule*, as in "home rule," and *roulard*). Freud ventures that the more alien the two circles of ideas brought together in this way, the greater the economy in psychological effort afforded by the technique and the more intense the pleasure. Because in this case the interlinked circles of ideas are connected only by sound, that is, an external association, Freud continues, the home-roulade joke is a bad one (though not necessarily bad *as* a joke, p. 146n), verging on a mere jest. The joke discussed earlier in this chapter, *Traduttore—Traditore*, deploys the resonance of sound to signal a conceptual connection ("translators are traitors") and thus forms a more elevated form of joking. It affords a different and perhaps more sublime pleasure.

A second cluster of techniques subsumes a variety of devices, among them plays on similarity of sound, multiple use of the same material, the modification of familiar phrases and the allusion to famous quotations. All of these devices embody the rediscovery of something familiar where one might have expected something new. Examples include *Le roi n'est pas sujet*, already cited, or "It is almost impossible to carry the torch of truth through a crowd without singeing someone's beard" (from Lichtenberg, cited in Freud, 1905/1989, 97). The rediscovery of the familiar saves the psychical expenditure that might have been deployed in processing something new. Thus the pleasure in the rediscovery of the familiar could embody a pleasure in economy (p. 148). A similar pleasure might arise from jokes that highlight the act of remembering in itself, which, according to Freud, forms the core of topical jokes (p. 149).

The third category of techniques encompasses faulty thinking, absurdity, and other manifestations of "pleasure in nonsense" (1905/1989, 153), where the "nonsense" does not necessarily employ the devices of repetition and unification just noted. The joke about the inebriated tutor is an example. Like the replacement of conceptual connection with a sound-association in the first group of techniques, the third group of maneuvers economizes on psychical expenditure in the relaxation of the rules of disciplined thought.

One can discern from this analysis how tendentious jokes would, as a rule, produce a greater yield of pleasure than would innocent jokes. Tendentious jokes employ the same techniques as do innocent jokes and add another source of economization to them. The sum of these sources, Freud adds following the psychophysicist Gustav Fechner (1897), may greatly exceed the pleasure derived from the parts (Freud, 1905/1989, 165).

This codification of techniques highlights another property common to all the techniques and hence integral to the economization Freud believes they embody. Each type of technique represents a characteristic of childhood mentation. In doing so, it further embodies a "saving" in mental expenditure by casting off the burden imposed by subsequent development. The first group of techniques links words through sound at the expense of meaning, a method evident in children's early word learning and word play and rejected by serious thought. The third group, consisting of faulty reasoning, absurdity, and so on, again reverts to a mode of thought that does not care about logical rigor. In capitalizing upon the rediscovery of the familiar, the middle group of techniques reverts to a signature pastime of childhood. As Freud notes here and elsewhere (e.g., 1920/1989), children thrive upon repetition and derive intense pleasure from it. Babies shake their rattles or enjoy someone's funny faces over and over again. Children want to hear the same story far more times than adult interest would ever sustain. People of all ages, and especially children, derive in addition a comfort in the familiar, as against the anxiety that can be provoked by the unknown or less known (Freud, 1905/1989, 148).

Joking, Freud continues in addressing development, begins as verbal and conceptual play of the sort just described: what we adults would describe as empty sound associations, repetitions without clear meaning or augmentation, absurdity or logical sleights of hand without purpose. As Freud envisions the development, critical judgment gradually supervenes and eventually rejects the earlier play as meaningless. The earlier effects are enjoyed once again only when they arise accidentally or when growing youths, or adults, become overtaken by a pleasurable mood that, like a child's cheerfulness, lifts their critical inhibition (1905/1989, 157): "Standards of joking sink as spirits rise," says Freud (p. 155).

But, Freud says, we also search for ways to bring on these pleasures ourselves. We do this by maneuvering to avoid the criticism that would otherwise bar the play. We accomplish the maneuver by inserting a message into the mix. The jest, which Freud conceives as the first step beyond verbal and conceptual play, says something—anything—decorum permits. It says it regardless of whether the content has any value or whether the resulting form would strike the dispassionate listener as particularly good. Freud cites as an illustration the remark by the eighteenth-century physics professor Kästner, who had asked the age of a new student of his named Kreigk and learned it was thirty: "Ah! So I have the honor of meeting the Thirty Years' War [*Krieg*]" (from Kleinpaul, 1890; cited in Freud, 1905/1989, 158). Or, upon being asked the professions of his four sons, the nineteenth-century Viennese anatomist Carl Rokitansky is said to have replied, "Two ***heilin*** [heal] and two ***heulen*** [howl]"; two are doctors and two are singers (Freud, 1905/1989, 159). Admitting a barely perceptible line between jests and jokes, Freud says these examples impart simply accurate, inoffensive information that becomes humorous, and thus pleasurable, only because of the form in which it is imparted. The content affords a pretext for descending into the old play with words and thoughts and obviates the need for criticism that might otherwise intervene (p. 159).

Once a jest contains substance and value, Freud continues, it becomes a joke (1905/1989, 161). At that juncture, the joking envelope can bribe one's critical powers into accepting otherwise inadmissible content. The means by which this happens is that in the total impression of pleasure left by the joke one cannot discern the contributions, respectively, of the joke's form and its content (p. 161). Thus, at bottom, we do not know what we are laughing at (p. 162).

If the object of joking is enjoyment, and the source of the enjoyment the savings of energy afforded by both the release from inhibition and the mental work saved by joke techniques, the question remains of why jokes provoke laughter specifically. Laughter is a pleasurable response of a particular kind. It is an explosive discharge, by contrast with the more measured release realized in something like a sigh, which can also signal a relief from tension and the accession to pleasure. Also in need of explanation is the circumstance that the laughter manifests not in the teller of the joke, but in its hearer.

The explanation of the latter effect provides leverage on the first question, of why laughter is the result of (successful) joking. Freud extrapolates that the reason why the hearer, but not the teller, of a joke laughs cannot be that only one of them—the hearer—experiences a lifting of inhibition. Were tellers to experience no lifting of inhibition, the joke could not come about; thus they must have their inhibitions lifted as well. The difference must arise instead in the possibilities for discharge of the effort now no longer needed. Freud surmises that the production of the joke itself attenuates the energy available to the teller for discharge. The hearer, meanwhile, receives the joke ready-made. Provided the hearer's comprehension of the joke requires no extra effort, and the joke succeeds in evoking the relevant inhibitions in the hearer, then the hearer is positioned to find the inhibitions superfluous just as they are forming: *in statu nascendi*, as Freud says, borrowing a term from G. Heymans (1896), who used it somewhat differently in his theory of the comic. The hearer then "laughs off" the extra "quota" of energy (Freud, 1905/1989, 182), much as one's arm flies into the air when one lifts an item one expected to be heavy that turns out to be light. Tellers, who lack the resources for discharge, now achieve their pleasure vicariously, through the hearer, in whom the discharge is realized.

Freud next deepens his search for mechanism, motivated by the close correspondence he has observed between joke techniques and the properties of dreamwork for which he found evidence in his extensive analysis of dreams (1900/1965). Like jokes, the elements of dreams condense several thoughts into one, represent ideas by their opposites or by nonsense, use indirect representation, and fray logic. Given the affiliation of dreams with the unconscious, Freud extrapolates that jokes, also, may draw from the unconscious. He conceives the contribution as a momentary giving over of what he calls preconscious thought to unconsious revision. By *preconscious thought* he means thought that could be conscious were one attending to it. The results of the unconscious revision are immediately grasped by conscious perception (1905/1989, 205). He cites as additional evidence for the possible interplay of unconscious processing in jokes: a correlation he had suspected earlier might exist between joking ability and neurosis (p. 174); the impression that people's production of a joke begins with an *absence* (the French term) after which the joke seems to erupt fully formed (p. 207); and the brevity of jokes (p. 208f).

But unconscious processes reduce at bottom to modalities of child thought, and all the distinguishing characteristics Freud identifies in dreams, and now jokes, appear in children's thought activity. Thus, Freud infers, a thought in the process of transforming into a joke via a plunge into the unconscious is being remanded to the person's intellectual childhood. The result, and presumably the intent, of the return is the regaining of the sources of pleasure there (p. 210).

Childhood figures still more prominently in Freud's analysis of species of the comic beyond jokes, with which he concludes his study. The comic proper, he says, is found, rather than made, or at least it need not be made, and, as found, can dispense with the extra person to whom its results need to be told. One can laugh heartily at a display one finds comic without needing to impart it to an external party. Nonetheless, given that laughter results, Freud must now find a way to extend his account of the genesis of laughter to a process different from that of jokes—the account of the genesis of laughter being that one "laughs off" a surplus of energy just as it is being deployed (i.e., *in statu nascendi*).

The comic of the naïve stands closest to jokes, Freud thinks, and realizes most completely the condition of being found, rather than made. It must arise in a setting in which the comedy is not in any way intended. It resides in an act or effect that would normally be subject to inhibition on the observer's part, but is executed by the actor free of any inhibition. It lacks inhibition not because the inhibition is circumvented, but because it is simply not present. The result, therefore, is understood to arise without any effort on the actor's part. It is important that the observer know the actor does not possess the inhibition, because were the actor perceived to possess the inhibition, the actor would come across as impudent, rather than naïve. The observer would feel indignation rather than mirth (Freud, 1905/1989, 226). Under the appropriate conditions, then, laughter results when the inhibition the observer would normally deploy, now aroused empathically, becomes superfluous in the same or immediately succeeding moment and is laughed off. In this result, the observer behaves like hearers of a joke who are presented with a ready-made economization on inhibition and consequently can then laugh off their own habitual inhibition (p. 53, preceding).

Given that inhibitions emerge with development, the naïve comic arises most frequently in children, who do not yet know the inhibitions that would obstruct an adult's delivery of the same behavior. Freud gives as an example a three-and-a-half-year-old girl's warning to her brother that he would get some *Bubizin* if he became ill. She had evidently extrapolated from the fact that she had been given *Medizin*, which she understood as *Mädi-zin*, so named because she was a little girl (*Mädi*), that the treatment for a little boy (*Bubi*) was *Bubi-zin* (1905/1989, 226). The construction follows the format of a verbal joke employing the technique of similarity of sound. As Freud suggests, the same thing could occur as a joke, which, he anticipates, would be met perhaps with mild pleasure. It raises a laugh as a piece of naïveté. The difference, he offers, lies in the observer's perception that the child's remark was not intended as a joke and arose rather as an effort at a serious conclusion.

A second example offers the equivalent in the comic naïve of a tendentious joke. Performing a two-part play of their own design, a ten- and twelve-year-old brother and sister enacted first a scene in which a poor fisherman decides to leave his devoted and honest wife to seek his fortune elsewhere. The second act opens with his return a few years later sporting a large bag of money and declaiming his good luck to his wife, who has met him outside their hut. She interrupts him to announce proudly, "I too have not been idle," whereupon she opens the door to the hut and reveals twelve dolls asleep on the floor. At this point the audience of otherwise demure relatives interrupted with a burst of laughter the actors could not comprehend. One supposes that here, as in the first example, the laughter presupposes the absence of any humorous intent in the actors, that absence predicated, in turn, upon their ignorance of the assumptions that would have rendered the scene humorous to the onlookers (Freud, 1905/1989, 227–28).

Examples of this kind lead Freud to the formula for laughter at the naïve comic: Receivers experience empathically the absence of inhibition in the producer by putting themselves into the producer's mental process in bringing about the display. At the same time they experience the process through which the display would have arisen in them, which in the two examples noted would have required the surmounting of an inhibition. If receivers elect to understand the producer, they recognize they can economize on the psychical expenditure they would need to keep up the barrier that would intrude upon their production of the same thing. The expenditure thus "liberated" provides the source of pleasure in the naïve and is discharged by laughter (Freud, 1905/1989, 231–32).

Other varieties of the comic, such as mimicry, unmasking, caricature, and pantomime, likewise derive, on Freud's analysis, from the difference in psychical expenditure one experiences in comparing one's own and another's expenditure when one tries to understand the other. In the case of the naïve, the expenditure is saved on inhibition, and it is on account of that feature that the naïve comes closest among varieties of the comic to jokes. In other cases, such as pantomime, as seen for instance in clowns, the expenditure attaches to intellectual or physical effort. Comic effects can also arise when not enough effort is put into something; Freud suggests that people appear comical who put too much expenditure into bodily functions and too little into mental ones (1905/1989, 242). If, on the other hand, he notes, we perceive the other person to make a smaller physical expenditure or a greater mental one than we would make in the same situation, then rather than laugh, we become filled with awe and admiration (p. 242).

Although we may find children comical, and may also retrieve childhood pleasures in our appreciation of jokes and the comic, the relation of the comic to children is complex. Therefore, so is the psychological composition of the adult capacity. Children in themselves do not strike us as comical, Freud remarks, when, for instance, they kick or jump about and otherwise act like children (1905/1989, 235). They produce a comic effect on us only when we end up comparing their expenditure of energy with the expenditure we would make in the same situation. Then the conditions of the comic strike us: the extra expenditure on movement, the small expenditure on thought, the domination of bodily over mental function, and more (p. 277).

We find it comical, for instance, when a child learning to write sticks out his tongue as he moves the pen, because we understand the activity as one of ours and thus envision how we would carry it out, namely, with less movement (Freud, 1905/1989, 235). Similarly, Freud adds, the passionate movements of modern conductors may strike those uneducated in music as comical insofar as they do not understand the necessity of the movements. They would exert themselves less to do the same thing (p. 236).

Thus, to find children comical, we must observe them either performing an activity normally executed by adults or otherwise endeavoring to behave as serious adults, as did the brother and sister who presented the play. These conditions will provoke in us the necessary comparison. Otherwise, says Freud, we derive pure pleasure from our observation of children, accompanied perhaps by at most a reminder of the comic (1905/1989, 277).

Children, conversely, lack a feeling for the comic themselves until they perceive differences in expenditure between their own efforts and someone else's in their attempt to understand the other person. Initially, however, they draw no comparison, or they mimic the other. Upbringing soon introduces the standard of how some things ought to be done. Thereafter children can apply the standard to their appraisal of others. They can reach the judgment, "He did not do it right," or "I can do it better" (Freud, 1905/1989, 278). But, Freud discerns, the resulting laughter, should it arise, would constitute laughter at the person, rather than laughter at the comic (p. 278). It would be the laughter of derision, the sort that would have emerged if the relatives witnessing the play by the brother and sister had laughed at the ignorance of the actors instead of at the comedy the relatives perceived. It is the laughter of superiority and, as such, an expression of pure pleasure, rather than a manifestation of a feeling for the comic.

Freud extrapolates further that children probably laugh from pure pleasure in many circumstances that we would find comical. In these instances the motives of our laughter are wrapped to some degree in obscurity, whereas children's motives are clear. If someone slips and falls in the street, a child may laugh from a feeling of superiority or malicious pleasure, as if to say, "You've fallen down, I haven't" (Freud, 1905/1989, 278–79). If we laugh, we do so because we find the scene comical, though, if pressed, we would not be able to say exactly why.

Like authors on the subject before him, Freud perceives in comic laughter the lost laughter of childhood momentarily regained. Into this account he interpolates a verbalization of the experience: "I laugh at a difference in expenditure between another person and myself every time I rediscover the child in him," or, more exactly, "That is how he does it—I do it another way—he does it as I used to do it as a child" (1905/1989, 279). It does not matter in this comparison whether the comic display entails a greater or a smaller expenditure than the adult would make. All that matters is the perception of a difference, and, Freud says, though he later wavers on the point (p. 283), the comic falls invariably on the infantile side of the comparison (p. 279). He finds compatible with this account his previous observation that children themselves, behaving as children, need not produce a comic impression. They are behaving as they ought to do and therefore provide no occasion for comparison (of expenditure). Someone who gives a comic impression is behaving in a way that evokes a comparison of expenditures: either a child behaves as an adult or an adult behaves in a less expeditious way than one would expect of an adult.

Freud clarifies, then, that the comic need not recoup old childish pleasures in particular, but childish nature in general (1905/1989, 280). Yet it entails more than this revival. It results from a comparison made possible only by development, in which the same thing is looked at from two vantage points, of which but one is the child's.

If jokes dispel an inhibition and the comic an intellectual expenditure *in statu nascendi*, then humor, the third and final category of the broadly comic Freud considers, disarms an affect in the process of mobilization. Gallows humor, for instance, neutralizes the suffering we envision the condemned to be experiencing or the pity we are prepared to feel on their behalf. "Well, this week's beginning nicely," comments the scoundrel of Freud's opening example on the way to the gallows (1905/1989, 284; see also Freud, 1927a/1985). Also a joke, the remark stands as a piece of humor insofar as the joke is made by someone who will not live to see the week finish and who by rights ought to be experiencing anything other than a nice start to the week. Instead he disregards the distinction between this week and others (p. 285). Similarly with the scamp en route to execution who asks for a scarf to cover his throat so he will not catch cold. A worthy precaution under other circumstances, it is undermined in this case by the imminent fate of the man's neck. We laugh when either the despair we begin to build on the man's behalf or the pity we start to muster toward him are turned to naught (p. 285).

The economy of pity or at least piety forms the basis of much of Mark Twain's humor, according to Freud. In one of Twain's vignettes, for example, Twain presents his family tree, which he traces to one of Columbus' voyagers. He comes in the course of the account to dwell upon how the ancestor's baggage consisted of numerous pieces of wash, each bearing a different laundry mark. Freud says we laugh at this juncture in the story at the sudden superfluity of the piety into which we have been drawn by the beginning of the story (1905/1989, 286).

As he does with jokes and the comic, Freud identifies a childhood source of humor to which, however, like jokes and the (narrowly) comic, humor does not reduce. Humor, he says, is the highest form of psychological defense. It protects the ego from distressing or otherwise oppressive affect. Unlike defensive mechanisms such as denial or repression, which do away with the offending content and thus begin the descent toward pathology, however, humor retains the content in consciousness. It finds the means to divert the energy from the unpleasure building up in connection with the content and changes it, by discharging it, into pleasure (1905/1989, 290). Freud speculates that this transformation is effected by humorists' comparison of their adult and childish ego. In the normal run of things, children become distressed by matters adults find trivial. In turning a distressing situation into a humorous one, adults project the distressing affect onto the childish ego and smile at the smallness of the worry as viewed from an adult perspective. In his later paper on humor (1927a/1985), Freud adds that in this exchange we coddle ourselves, as a parent might a child, as if to say all will be well and there is nothing to worry about.

In all the varieties of the comic Freud has considered, pleasure arises, according to the account, from an economy on the psychical work we do, granted the delicate timing of capturing the work *in statu nascendi*. In jokes we economize on an inhibition, in the comic proper on ideation, and in humor on feeling. In each venue, we achieve this economy through the re-evocation of sources of mental pleasure we have lost through the development of our mental life. In this resurrection, we are re-creating the mood of a period in our lives when we naturally dealt with our psychical work with small expenditures of mental energy, when, Freud adds, we were "ignorant of the comic, incapable of jokes, and had no need of humor to make us feel happy in our life" (1905/1989, 293).

At the heart of the adult capacity for the comic, broadly conceived, then, lie the proclivities of a child, as these have been transformed by the layers of mental life added by development. Our capacity for the comic embodies our childish selves, but only we, and not children, have the capacity. One must understand both sides of this formula, in all their ramifications, to understand this part of human mental life.

NOTES

1. In a footnote added in 1912, Freud notes the correction that the joke appears to have been used earlier by Heine to describe Alfred de Musset.

2. The English editor of Freud's text notes that the term of abuse in German is *Vieh* which means more generally "animal."

Chapter Eight

The Experience of the "Uncanny": "The 'Uncanny'" (1919)

In his treatment of the experience of the uncanny, Freud (1919/1985) again conceives both childhood and one's development past it as fundamental to an adult capacity, and it is once again the interaction of our childlike and adult selves that produces the capacity. This time, however, Freud devotes attention to the manner in which development occurs and the possibility of different developmental dynamics coming into play. Further, in the case of the uncanny, Freud constructs a psychology of a passive experience, as opposed to one we produce.

Feelings are not easy to study. Normally one experiences them and can say little about what the feeling entails. Yet where language provides a discrete term for a cluster of such experiences, one must assume a discrete core of sensibility exists and that most people recognize the sensibility when it arises in them, even if they cannot describe it. The "uncanny," as Freud's original *unheimliche* is translated, is such a category. It verges on the frightening and what excites dread and horror and yet exists apart, for it has its own term in numerous languages. One wants to know what warrants the term.

Remarkably, even though he claims not to have experienced the feeling himself, Freud manages in the course of his analysis to give the feeling pointed articulation, such that one walks away from his exposition immersed in the feeling, regardless of whether one feels persuaded by his explanation of it. For example, although one may disparage Freud's hypothesis that the idea of being robbed of one's eyes evokes an uncanny feeling because of repressed castration anxiety, one may simultaneously begin to feel a sense of the uncanny in reading his analysis. I continue with a reconstruction of Freud's account, aimed at identifying its basic constituents and tracking in particular his juxtaposition of child and adult in the unpacking of the experience.

Freud draws upon two converging lines of evidence to identify the distinguishing characteristics of the uncanny. One is the linguistic history of *unheimliche*, and the other an open-ended search for common denominators in people's experience of the feeling. The result, he presages, is an account of the uncanny as a subcategory of the frightening that leads back to what is known of old and long familiar. He conceives it as the task of his presentation to show how this paradoxical result can come about, given that we are disposed to imagine the familiar as comforting, like home.

Unheimlich derives from *heimlich*, originally meaning of the home or family, of which it forms the opposite. One is therefore tempted to conclude that *unheimlich* refers to what is frightening on account of its lack of familiarity. However, given that not everything that is novel and unfamiliar is frightening, Freud reasons, the uncanny must entail something in addition to the unfamiliar.

Tracing the history of *heimlich*, he shows that the term shades into its opposite, *unheimlich*. In one meaning cited by one of his sources, a given family is compared with "a buried spring or dried up pond. One cannot walk over it without always having the feeling that water might come up there again," or "Oh, we call it 'unheimlich'; you call it 'heimlich.' Well, what makes you think there is something secret and untrustworthy about this family?" (Freud, 1919/1985, 343–44). And

"'Unheimlich' is the name for everything that ought to have remained . . . secret and hidden but has come to light" (p. 345, ellipsis in original). Later still, from the Grimms' dictionary (1877), Freud cites, "From the idea of 'homelike,' 'belonging to the house,' the further idea is developed of something withdrawn from the eyes of strangers, something concealed, secret" (p. 346). *Unheimlich*, Freud says, thus emerges as a subcategory of *heimlich* and not merely as its opposite.

Freud opens his exploration of the experience of the uncanny with a retelling of E. T. A. Hoffmann's story "The Sandman" (Hoffman, 1952), which arouses an uncanny feeling in many readers and formed the object of the one previous psychological investigation into the uncanny of which Freud was aware when he wrote his piece. The previous author, Ernst Jentsch, ascribed the feeling of uncanniness to intellectual doubt as to whether an entity is a human or automaton. He believed the feeling was evoked in Hoffmann's tale by the reactions of the protagonist, the student Nathaniel, to the mechanical, life-sized doll Olympia, whom he believed to be alive. But, Freud points out, the story, like many other works of Hoffmann's, evokes the uncanny pervasively with other imagery that has nothing to do with the blurring of the distinction between the living and the nonliving.

The story begins with Nathaniel's recollections from childhood of the tale of the Sandman, an evil person who threw sand into the eyes of children who refused to go to bed, such that the eyes would jump out bleeding, to be carried away by the Sandman to feed his children. Often, after bedtime, Nathaniel would hear the heavy tread of an unidentified visitor to his beloved father and whom he associated with the storied Sandman.

One evening, having decided to keep watch to determine the visitor's identity, Nathaniel discovers the visitor to be the lawyer Coppelius, whom he and his siblings have always found repulsive and fearsome. As his father and Coppelius work at a flaming brazier, Nathaniel hears Coppelius call out, "Eyes here! Eyes here!" and screams, exposing himself. Coppelius grabs him, threatening to drop hot coal into his eyes, but the father intervenes. Nathaniel faints and succumbs to a long illness.

Now in remission and a university student, Nathaniel believes Coppelius has reemerged in the figure of Giuseppe Coppola, a traveling optician who sells weather glasses and from whom Nathaniel, initially terrified, buys a small spyglass. With the instrument he gazes at the house opposite and catches sight of the owner's beautiful but silent and motionless daughter, Olympia. Nathaniel falls violently in love with the creature, to the neglect of the wise and sensible Clara, to whom he is engaged. Olympia, however, is a mechanical doll her "father" Spalanzani has made; her eyes have been furnished by Coppola, the Sandman-Coppelius.

Nathaniel, hoping to meet Olympia, ventures to Spalanzani's house and comes upon Spalanzani and Coppola arguing over their creation, her eyes lying bleeding on the floor. As Coppola carries off the inert figure, Spalanzani throws the bleeding eyes at Nathaniel, telling him Coppola had stolen them from Nathaniel. Succumbing to a new attack of madness, Nathaniel sets upon Spalanzani and attempts to strangle him.

Later, recovered, Nathaniel reconciles with Clara and plans to marry her. But before long yet another sighting of Coppelius propels Nathaniel into madness, this time atop a tower from which he attempts unsuccessfully to hurl Clara and then succeeds in hurling himself. Coppelius meanwhile vanishes in the crowd below.

Granted that one might experience intellectual uncertainty about whether the wooden doll, Olympia, is alive and possibly also a sense of uncanniness in consequence, a sense of the uncanny pervades the story and is evoked more strikingly by other images. It attaches particularly, Freud says, to the idea of being robbed of one's eyes. Through a review of other evidence and further analysis, Freud links the dread of loss of the eyes to the fear of castration. Important to our purpose is neither this claim nor its basis, but the observation that this repeated ingredient of the story, the loss of the eyes, arouses uncanniness and does so independently of any confusion between the living and the mechanical. The image remains uncanny, moreover, regardless of whether one perceives the story to move in reality or in fantasy.

Additional ingredients of the story that arouse uncanniness include the reappearance of the same, in this case evil, character in different guises: the figure of the Sandman, Coppelius, and Coppola. Following the research of his disciple Otto Rank, Freud observes that in a much earlier historical period, people held the idea of a "double," a copy of oneself, to be an insurance against death. Thus they believed the soul, understood as the "double" of the body, assured a continuation of life after death and conceived guardian spirits, shadows, one's likeness in the mirror, and other such images as emblems of good things. In the same vein, the ancient Egyptians made images of the dead in lasting material, to preserve those loved and admired.

Freud connects the idea of the double as insurance against the destruction of the ego—in other words, against death—to primary narcissism, the phase of unbounded love Freud ascribes to both human history and individual human development. When this stage is superseded, however, the double takes on the opposite meaning. It becomes the harbinger of death, something alien to the ego, something uncanny. Freud surmises that the special quality of uncanniness attached to the double derives from the circumstance that the double is a creation that dates back to an earlier period of mental life, a period in which it wore a friendlier "aspect" (1919/1985, 358), and that this period has been superseded. What is uncanny is an experience that reawakens an old belief, or in some cases an old feeling or fantasy, where the belief, and so forth, has been superseded.

Freud draws an intriguing distinction here between two different ways in which an earlier disposition can become superseded and its value thereby transformed. It may be "surmounted," as in the case of the double, in the sense that an ordinary, universal stage of development is supplanted by another. Alternatively, it may be repressed, a mechanism, as we have discussed, that operates on individual experiences, pushing them from consciousness on account of their perceived threat; the impulses remain active in the unconscious where they may continue to exert influence on conscious life, though typically in distorted form. Freud ascribes the uncanniness of the loss of the eyes to the mechanism of repression, castration anxiety specifically. The mechanism of surmounting accounts for the more readily recognizable and more pervasive instances of the uncanny and represents the type of developmental explanation of concern to this book.

Freud believes other forms of uncanniness, besides the idea of the double, also date back to early ego feeling, including, for example, the involuntary repetition of an action, the prompt fulfillment of wishes, and other coincidences. He cites as instances of involuntary repetition his inadvertent return to the red-light district in an unfamiliar town when he was trying to arrive elsewhere, or one's return to the same place when one is lost in the woods and is attempting to get out. Or one continues to encounter the same number in different venues in a short period of time, for instance, one receives tag number sixty-two in the cloakroom and then on the bakery queue, and then discovers the number on a returned letter one misaddressed. Anything reminiscent of what Freud calls the inner "compulsion to repeat" (p. 360; see also 1920/1989 for further details) can evoke the feeling of uncanniness.

Freud cites as an example of the prompt fulfillment of wishes the incident in which the young lieutenant of his "Rat Man" case (1909a/1963) said he wished dead the old man occupying the room at a spa he desired for himself so he could resume relations with the nurse who had the room next door. The old man had a stroke shortly after. An instance of a different coincidence would be one's unexpected encounter with just the person of whom one had been thinking. The young lieutenant coined the term *omnipotence of thoughts* to describe the uncanny feeling he experienced upon the fulfillment of his so-called wish. The idea bears the stamp of animistic thought and hence of narcissism, the early developmental stage through which everyone passes.

It is only after the development of this analysis that Freud is able to find the words with which to represent the feeling of the uncanny. When the feeling of the uncanny arises in response to the apparent confirmation of a surmounted belief, it is as though, Freud says, we were making the judgment, "So, after all, it is *true* that one can kill a person by the mere wish!" while another part of us says it isn't possible (1919/1985, 371, emphasis in the original).

To situate more fully Freud's claim that the feeling of uncanniness derives from a clash of more primitive and more developed beliefs, we may usefully contrast the adult reaction in the foregoing instances with the reaction of babies and small children to equivalent events. Babies delight in action-reaction sequences one might describe as magical from their point of view. They shake a rattle, and it sounds. They pound their legs, and the toys hanging over the crib move. They squeal, and Dad pops up at the end of the crib. Before they understand the detailed causal relations that bring about these effects, babies note simply the correspondence between their movements and an outcome. They feel a terrific sense of efficacy as a result, according to Freud and many others, including the late Swiss psychologist Jean Piaget (e.g., 1937/1954), who provided detailed observations of the behavior. And they cannot have enough of these events. They repeat them over and over again and rejoice if the events are repeated for them.

Importantly in the present context, sequences of this kind do not bother babies in the least. They delight in them. By contrast, if *we* pound the table and a parakeet mysteriously appears at the other end of it, the result is no longer pleasurable, but uncanny. If, while brushing our teeth one morning, we suddenly think of a friend from high school with whom we subsequently lost touch and then run into her at the bus depot, we experience a feeling of the uncanny, even if also pleasure.

As yet unstudied, but worth inquiry, is the question of when in the course of their development children become prone to the experience of the uncanny. Many children engage in magical procedures by the time they enter school: skipping cracks in the sidewalk to assure a wanted outcome or to avoid an unwanted one, wishing for the opposite of what they want so as to get it, counting to ten between rattles of the radiator or thunderbolts to avert disaster. Were their wishes to come true, repeatedly, would they feel only joy at a happy conclusion or uncanniness at a bizarre occurrence that, to their current way of thinking, ought not to have occurred?

In one published anecdote on the experience of the uncanny in children, the British psychologist James Sully (1895/2000) reports an instance in which a baby of ten months showed excessive fear on returning to his nursery after a month away, whereas he showed no discomfort upon being placed in a strange nursery. At thirteen months, he seemed pleased to come home after two weeks' absence, the result, his mother suggested, of a strengthening of his memory (p. 200). Sully speculates that partial recognition gave the baby a sense of the uncanny, akin to adults' experience when a place seems familiar and they cannot recall having seen it before. Sully's example concerns the revitalization of a visual perception, as opposed to the resuscitation of a discarded belief, and thus makes difficult any generalization to the question of when uncanniness of the sort Freud describes is first experienced. However, it does echo the portion of Freud's argument that ascribes the feeling of uncanniness to a reanimated experience of the past whose reality is in doubt.

The contrast between babies' and adults' experience of the same kind of event suggests that the capacity to feel the uncanny is at least somewhat delayed and could therefore engage a dynamic of the sort Freud describes. It is an inherent part of feeling the uncanny that an event is processed as a recurrence of something more archaic revisited through the lens of current ideation. One cannot look only at the experience itself to understand it. One must take into account its developmental location, as modified by the transformation either of surmounting or repression. Experiences that were initially pleasurable may recur later, but with a completely different subjective quality, owing to the further development of the mind.

Freud's claim is that we have original experiences that can and do recur later, after they have undergone significant modification by the mind. At least two importantly different kinds of modification can occur, one through repressing and the other through surmounting. In either case, if the original experience recurs, the episode that awakens it will be perceived as uncanny.

It is intriguing that Freud's argument here takes the shape of something on the order of a proof: An experience of the uncanny cannot arise *unless* a developmental interaction of the sort he describes occurs. In contemporary psychology, connections between earlier and later developments are typically inferred on weaker grounds. One identifies what appear to be antecedents to some mature ability on the basis of similarities the observer discerns between the two behaviors or, occasionally, training effects of the earlier on the later behavior.

But the developmental link investigators are wont to infer between the earlier and later performances can be shown to be arbitrary. Mature, reflective concepts could arise in a more piecemeal fashion from what is claimed, for instance, rather specifically as differentiations, falsifications, or appropriations of the children's earlier, inchoate views (see Sugarman, 1987). Freud's argument from logical necessity at least has the form of something more than a descriptive parallel or other association in the observer's mind.

Chapter Nine

The Paradox of Surprise in the Face of Certainty: "A Disturbance of Memory on the Acropolis" (1936)

The summer of 1904 found Freud, then forty-eight, traveling on vacation to Athens with his younger brother. When Freud arrived at last atop the Acropolis and gazed at his surroundings, the surprising thought, as he later described it, suddenly occurred to him: "So all this really *does* exist, just as we learned at school!" (1936b/1984, 449, emphasis in the original English. The original German: *Also existiert das alles wirklich so wie wir es auf der Schule gelernt haben*?! [Freud, 1936a/1950, 251]).

It was as if, as he was to describe the experience later, he had been divided into two people. One of them felt obliged in the face of incontrovertible evidence to accept the reality of something whose existence he had previously found doubtful. This person responded, he later said, as someone might who had seen the Loch Ness monster creeping along the shore of the lake and felt compelled to confirm, "So it really *does* exist, the sea-serpent we've never believed in!" The second person, he says, felt incredulous that the existence of the Acropolis had ever been in doubt.

Puzzled over the years by how his mind could have produced this paradoxical outcome, he set out to analyze it in 1936, some thirty-two years after the incident. He presented the results of his analysis in a brief occasional piece entitled "A Disturbance of Memory on the Acropolis," which he wrote as an open letter to Romain Rolland, his correspondent six years earlier in his discussion of the "oceanic feeling" addressed in chapter 5 of this book.

I consider Freud's moment because the experience he describes is at least somewhat common and appears to be salutary. It also invites a developmental analysis and ultimately a comparison with the uncanny, jokes, and other matters we have considered as these emerge in Freud's analyses. Freud, however, neither discusses the general version of his experience nor dwells upon its positive cast. He limits his remarks instead to his own experience and conceives his experience, which he regarded as potentially idiosyncratic, as defensively tainted. Conceiving his episode more along a pathological model, he veers away from the dialogue with child mentation that anchors his analyses of the uncanny, jokes, and so forth. He does not in any way class the episode with these other phenomena. Indeed, this is one analysis of Freud's that strikes me as strained; even his own experience seems to lend itself more to analytic directions he adopted elsewhere. Given the potential in this case for expansion beyond Freud's contribution, his short piece furnishes a good point of departure for the elaboration of his techniques beyond his own applications, to which the remainder of the book is devoted.

Regarding the generality of Freud's experience on the Acropolis, people sometimes arrive at a place they felt sure existed and find themselves surprised to discover it really exists. "Not just a piece of literary self-indulgence after all," remarks a character in Penelope Lively's *Moon Tiger*, when he sees the Sphinx (1989, 108). Shortly before I departed for a long-planned trip to a mountainous region of which I had recently learned, friends showed me pictures of the region they had taken during their visit to the same area ten years earlier. Observing the close similarity between their pictures and the ones I had seen in the guidebook that had inspired my trip, I found myself struck by the thought, "It's *real*." My tickets and other arrangements already in hand, I had not doubted the reality of the place. The latter example suggests that the sudden epiphany confirming the reality of something whose existence one already assumed can arise in the face of fresh evidence of the object's existence that does not necessarily include the object itself, as well as in an encounter with the object.

In this discussion, I label as *Freud's thought* or *the thought* experiences of the kind I have described in which in the face of supposedly relevant evidence people profess surprise, as Freud did, at the existence of an object of whose existence they were certain. I confine consideration to sincere, moving experiences, imbued to some degree with a sense of strangeness and surprise in at least somewhat the manner in which Freud describes his experience. I exclude pejorative or sarcastic assertions of the thought, which allude to, rather than express, the experience. Unless I indicate otherwise, I mean by *Freud's thought* (etc.) the general experience, as opposed to Freud's own specific one. I begin, however, with a reconstruction of Freud's analysis of his own experience.

Freud begins the analysis with a consideration of the way common sense might account for his thought on the Acropolis—"all this really does exist, just as we learned at school!"—expressed as though this were a revelation. Thus, one might suppose, he says, the thought expressed the sentiment that seeing something is different from hearing or reading about it. Even if he did experience this sentiment, the thought would remain a strange way of conveying this idea. It asserts that all this exists, not that all this looks different from the way Freud expected it to look.

He considers the ostensibly deeper alternative that although he thought he had believed in the reality of the Acropolis, perhaps he had unconsciously doubted it. Without elaborating, he finds this account beyond proof and questionable on theoretical grounds.

At this juncture, Freud leaves off superficial interpretation of the thought and begins to query other aspects of his experience on the trip that might afford clues to the motives of the thought. He notes an odd depression he and his brother experienced when, at the outset of their travels, they stopped in Trieste and made the decision to journey to Athens, rather than to Corfu, their original destination. Having warmed to the change in plans and decided to adopt it, they mused dispiritedly upon the impracticality of the trip and the obstacles that might prevent it. Nonetheless, when the ticket office opened selling passage on the boat they were to take, they proceeded without ado to make their purchase, as though they had never doubted they would do so. Looking back, Freud detects in the retrospectively senseless questioning in which he and his brother had engaged an incredulity that they were about to travel to Athens: "It's out of the question that we could see Athens! It would be far too difficult!" The accompanying depression they felt expressed the regret that they could not go, given that it would have been so lovely to do so (1936b/1984, 450). Thus, interprets Freud, they regarded the possibility of the trip as a prospect "too good to be true."

Scrutinizing next the idea of something being too good to be true, Freud concludes, based upon other analyses, that people sometimes repudiate welcome realities they feel they do not deserve (1936b/1984, 450–51). In Trieste, the brothers could not believe their good fortune that they might see Athens. Once they found themselves on the Acropolis, Freud extrapolates, the possibility had become reality, and the disbelief had only the actuality to attack. Given his humble and meager beginnings, he could not have imagined it possible that he would ever see Athens, and yet here he was.

Nonetheless, Freud observes, his thought on the Acropolis did not express incredulity at his having arrived there. It expressed dismay that the Acropolis is real, and it ascribed his incredulity not to the present moment, but to the past. He conceives machinations by which his mind might nonetheless have begun with his current incredulity about his arrival on the Acropolis and then transposed the feeling onto the Acropolis itself and projected the feeling into the past.

Given that he did not doubt the Acropolis' existence in the past, he speculates that the incredulity he expressed indeed did pertain to the present, and it pertained to the Acropolis. He was experiencing a "derealization," the feeling that the things around him were not real. Derealizations serve the purpose of defense: they keep something away from the ego that the ego cannot tolerate. Freud proposes that his derealization on the Acropolis repudiated his fulfillment of his long-standing wish to travel and see such places as Athens. These attainments implicitly denigrated his family and the conditions of his youth. Not only too poor to travel, Freud's father, who worked in business and had no secondary education, would not have appreciated the idea of going to Athens. Everyone believes it is wrong and forbidden to criticize or exceed one's parents. Hence Freud's need to repudiate his attainment.

Freud hypothesizes that he shifted his incredulity into the past because his mind could not account for the feeling of the unreal in the present, given that his senses were telling him his surroundings were real. In the past he had, however, doubted *something* about Athens, namely, whether he would ever see it. The memory provided him a means to shift his present sense of unreality into the past and thus make it more coherent. The result of the two transformations was an assertion that affirmed the previously dubious existence of the Acropolis, that is, the thought.

A separate study I completed (Sugarman, 1998) suggests Freud is correct that superficial readings of this type of the thought do not account for it. One can demonstrate this for oneself by following Freud's model of translating given readings of the thought into the assertion into which they would translate most directly and then seeing whether the assertion is the thought. For example, the superficial hypothesis Freud entertains, that "seeing something is different from hearing or reading about it," translates most directly into an assertion along the lines, "So this is what it looks like!"—which is not the thought.

Similarly with awe: Awe might translate most directly into expressions such as "Oh!" "Fantastic!" or "Amazing! *This* is what exists!" Freud's thought, however, affirms the reality of the Acropolis, as opposed to how it looks or feels.

Numerous other surface-level pretexts for the thought fall victim to the same shortcomings. They do not translate properly into Freud's thought. I have treated these alternatives at length elsewhere and curtail the exercise here, save to note that other quotidian thoughts yield more easily to the surface-level elaboration I have been illustrating (Sugarman, 1998, chapters 3 and 4).

Interestingly, in passing remarks he made on his thought ten years before he wrote his essay on it, Freud seems to suggest that absent the particular circumstances surrounding his experience, his thought on the Acropolis might have yielded to relatively straightforward explanation. He might have ascribed it, he says, to the fragility of the beliefs he had acquired as a child learning about faraway places.

He makes the remark in the context of his famous assault on religion in *The Future of an Illusion* (1927b/1989), where he chides religion for the unnaturalness and duplicity of the demand for faith without question. The teaching of geography, by contrast, commands belief, but produces grounds for its claims. One learns the earth has the shape of a sphere, for example, and learns proofs of this, such as Foucault's experiments with the pendulum, properties of the horizon, and the feasibility of traveling around the earth. Given that every schoolchild cannot circumnavigate the earth, people content themselves with taking many teachings on trust. However, Freud says, we know we may take additional steps to establishing personal conviction if we wish to do so. In this spirit, he cites a student song about the location of the town of Constance on the Bodensee, which concludes with "if you don't believe it go and see" (1927b/1989, 31–33). Uncomplicated by his circumstances, on this analysis, his thought would have given further evidence of this healthy skepticism.

Whether or not Freud would have proposed this analysis for the general case, the criticisms he levels at the "commonsense" accounts with which he opens his later essay would seem to apply to this earlier discussion. Even though one could approach much of what one knows with skepticism, the fact remains that, at the time one has Freud's thought, one has not recently entertained any skepticism about the existence of the thought's object. On the contrary, the slightest suggestion of prior doubt turns the experience into something else, namely, the terminus of problem-solving. As Freud says, it is part of the experience of having the thought that one be surprised one is having it.

The question thus remains of why one would return under this condition of certainty to the possibility of skepticism, and not only to the possibility of it, but to a distinct memory of having harbored it. Calling for accounting also in the class of cases we are considering, in which the thought emerges sincerely, is coincidence of the thought with a special feeling—of gladness, gratitude, revelation, or even what Freud describes as a derealization, the sense that the things around one are not real.

The insufficiency of face-value interpretation of the thought invites the search for a deeper account, and Freud's analysis offers a candidate. Even as an account solely of his own experience, as he intended the account, the analysis heads in a curious direction. It conceives the thought as a momentary pathology.

The account, in brief, is that Freud's guilt in reaching Athens—guilt of which he was unaware at the time—prompted a defensive process within him that resulted in his impression of the things around him as unreal, his derealization. His thought that the things around him indeed were real responded to this impression, but shifted it to the past, because of its conflict with his otherwise intact perception.

Granting the unease Freud felt surrounding his visit to Athens, the thought also joyously acknowledged his presence there. It could therefore have represented a lapse in his defense, rather than an extension of it, though we have as yet to conceive how it might have done this. Somewhat more peripherally, absent any further indication from Freud of severe anxiety attaching to the feeling of unreality he experienced, the idea seems odd that the feeling can have so disturbed him that it motivated any retracking of the feeling. The latter puzzle leaves obscure how he would have come to have a memory of previous uncertainty, to which the thought responded.

These problems become magnified when one tries to extend the account to the general case, granting, again, that Freud did not intend the account for the general case.

Even if the thought served as a defense whenever it occurs, the question would remain of why this defense is the one that arises. If everyone who has the thought has it, say, to deny a given point of arrival, numerous other evasions exist among which they might choose. One could think about the weather or the alignment of the columns on the Parthenon or one's plans for lunch. Why choose this defense in particular, and why would so many people choose it?

However, the question remains of what would motivate others' defensiveness upon their encounter with the real version of things of whose existence they had known. Freud remarks that his own circumstance may have been idiosyncratic (1927b/1989, 31–32). If others do not feel guilty, then the thought could not arise as a defense against guilt.

Above all, especially for the general case, one must question the faithfulness of the account to the subjective reality of the thought. The scenario Freud outlines, rooted in guilt and tinged by defensiveness, puts a negative cast on the experience that ultimately manifests in the thought. The thought seems rather more affirmatory, despite its allusion to a doubt. Once in Athens, you mount the Acropolis. There everything is. It really *does* exist! You not only have no awareness of any doubt, but take particular pleasure in your observation and feel release through it. These are not the qualities of defensively driven or otherwise burdened behavior.

The other analyses of Freud's we have been tracking until this point offer both tools for investigating the thought in a fresh direction and some ideas about its possible substance. I begin with a further elaboration of its subjective quality.

Not only affirmatory and pleasurable, Freud's thought is mundane. Given that its author has not doubted the existence of the thought's object and that, in the case of a well-known object such as the Acropolis, no one else would doubt it either, the thought asserts the obvious. All this that everyone knows exists, exists.

Together these qualities of the thought, its affirmatory and pleasurable nature and its mundanity, describe a *childlike* assertion. Children exult in what is obvious to adults, for it is not as obvious to them. Scant though this description may seem, it could supply the missing premise of the thought. Insofar as one affirms what appears to be obvious because it is not, in fact, obvious to one, the context for an affirmation exists. It is not obvious that "all this really exists." As Freud's own case exemplifies, adults, however, are capable of the thought, and an adult would not doubt that the Acropolis exists. Nevertheless, an adult could speak as a child, in the moment.

To establish whether adults might plausibly return to that vantage point when they have the thought, let us first examine more thoroughly the childlike point of view the thought might reflect.

Examples abound of instances in which children question, or as the case may be affirm, what is obvious to adults:[1]

A tour group visiting the South Street Seaport in New York City first examined the ship from the pier and then was taken on board. When the group reached the ship's deck, a child asked the guide, "Are we there?" Evidently she was unsure whether the object upon which she stood was the same thing she had seen from the pier. No adult would wonder. This kind of error is common among children. The parameters within which they recognize the same object or scene are narrower than are the parameters within which adults do so (Cole and Subbotsky, 1991; Harris, 1983; Piaget, 1937/1954).

Taking his first plane ride, a different child of four said to his father with combined relief and puzzlement, "Things don't really get smaller up here." He had seen planes only from the ground before (Matthews, 1980).

More generally, children revel in what we might call the rediscovery of the same thing in a new guise: seeing in real life a thing that has been talked about, discovering on a map or in a picture a place or object they have seen either in real life or in a different representation. "Banana!" cries a one-and-a-half-year-old girl when she runs to the refrigerator to point to a banana after having seen a picture of one in a book. Another girl of two goes to retrieve her wooden hippopotamus when she and a parent read about a hippo in a book. More generally, the matching of words to things preoccupies children in the second year (e.g., Brown, 1973), as does the collecting in both talk and play of discrete exemplars of the same type of thing (Sugarman, 1983). For an instance in which contact with the reality led to subsequent interest in its representation: After seeing a building burn during a family outing, a five-year-old boy became excited by pictures of the blaze he saw in the newspaper the next day.

The pleasure in reencountering things dates from our infancy. A baby's smiles register the recognition of the reappearance of the same, significant other people. As previous chapters have noted, babies also delight in reproducing the same effect themselves, and children can revisit the same spot, play the same game, or have the same story read to them countless times without the slightest decline in interest.[2] We may add to this list, babies' delight in peek-a-boo, where they find, lose, and rediscover the same people or things, the momentary loss heightening the thrill of recovery.

All these elements appear in Freud's thought. In addition to delivering the seemingly naïve affirmation of the existence of something whose existence an adult would normally take for granted, the thought arises during one's reencounter with something in a new guise. Freud learned about the Acropolis in school and then saw it one day. I learned from a guidebook of the mountain region I selected as a hiking destination and then saw similar images of it in friends' pictures.

Normally adults find the reencounter with the same thing, in the same or a different guise, routine and unremarkable. We read the work of a colleague and then meet the person. We hear of a sale on garden hoses and then go and buy one. Sometimes, however, even as adults we find reencounters with things or people we have known before exhilarating, as well as strange and disconcerting. We could find it exciting and strange to meet the very colleague, Jill P., whose work we had read. As we approach the hoses on the shelf, we could suddenly find it exhilarating to see and ultimately procure one of the hoses we saw advertised.

Meeting the same thing after any kind of lapse or change can stimulate and intrigue us in this way. Having hiked away from a country lake, we may find the view of it from the ridge we have reached gratifying, even if we knew we would see it. Although returning to our house or garage normally does not arouse us, it could do so, especially after a lapse such as a vacation.

This feeling of pleasure in reencountering things appears to depend upon our having lost touch with them at least briefly, just as the momentary disappearance of an object heightens a child's excitement in the object's return in peek-a-boo. The effect of sighting our lake again is diminished if we never lose sight of it as we mount the ridge. The experience is all the richer if we also have left off thinking about the lake during our ascent.

When people have Freud's thought, they experience the object of the thought, lose it or turn from it, and then regain it. They lose or turn from it in at least the sense that they do not think about it for a while. Freud learned about the Acropolis years before he saw it. I became enticed by the mountain region I had learned about, planned my trip there, and only several weeks later, upon learning my friends had gone there, saw the photos they had taken that prompted my surprised thought that the area was real.

A shorter interval can elapse between the initial and subsequent encounter: While listening to the radio one morning some years ago, I heard the station's weekly spot, "Inside the *New York Times* Best-Seller List." In the spot, the announcer briefly synopsizes the first few items on the list. On this occasion, my interest was mildly aroused by one of the titles. Later, while thumbing through the Book Review section of the paper, which carries the best-seller list, I turned to the list, as I often do, and found the title. For a moment I felt surprised to find it there. I had no recollection of having doubted the announcer and had not formulated any plan when having heard him to inspect the best-seller list for the book. I just found it strange and delightful, for a moment, to discover the title on the list.

The role of the familiar in our appreciation of things has been recognized at least since Aristotle, who explained the appeal of art in this way. When we have known the object of a painting before we see the painting, we enjoy what Aristotle called the imitative aspect of the painting (*mimesis*) and not only its technical execution (from *Poetics*; Aristotle, 1941, 4). The history of poetics has often revisited the theme that the artist performs precisely the mission of making the familiar strange again and hence of reinstating the "shock of recognition" (e.g., Pomorsky, 1987).

One may recognize another strand of childlike pleasure in Freud's thought in addition to the pleasure in recognition. One can detect in the thought the feeling of self-importance that can attend one's encountering an object of one's personal acquaintance.

In our adulthood and childhood, our participation in things makes them special. After watching the three-meter diving finals in the summer Olympics one evening, the next morning I enjoy reading about this competition in the newspaper more than I do reading about the competitions I did not see. My pleasure seems driven more by this reconnection than by the event in itself, which did not particularly interest me when I watched it. Strictly speaking, as news, this item should have held my interest least. I already knew about it.

One can imagine the reverse scenario: The day after one reads about a fire on the turnpike, one drives past the very location. It seems special, and one feels in a way pleased and proud, because one read about it.

In all of the instances that prompt Freud's thought, one encounters either an object or evidence of an object of which *one* knew earlier. The thought draws attention to this acquaintance in referring implicitly or explicitly to the object's existence "after all," which is to say, "just as *I* thought [learned, etc.]."

The pleasure and satisfaction we derive from the familiar and the urge to feel a part of things or feel our own importance never disappear, as we know from Freud. One can thus envision that, prompted by our arrival in a circumstance that stimulates this persisting piece of the child within, we might lapse for a moment into that child and affirm the obvious.

Nonetheless, Freud's thought, although perhaps childlike, is not something a child would normally think or say in the circumstances in which the thought arises in adults. Children affirm the existence, or other property, of something when its existence, or other property, has been in doubt. The child at the South Street Seaport did now know whether the boat on which she stood was the same one she had seen from the pier, and the boy who remarked that things did not really get smaller in an airplane was making a genuine discovery. Children argue over whether Santa is real or discuss whether there is a god. When they exult in their encounter with an item they have heard or read about, or discover a picture or other reference to something they have seen, they celebrate the reencounter. They do not affirm the object's real existence, unless, again, it has been in doubt. The child who ran to the refrigerator to locate a banana after having seen a picture of one shouted, "Banana!" The boy who gloried in the news story of the fire he had seen affirmed that this is what he had seen, not that it was real. He knew it was real.

One might wonder whether, when it occurs in adults, the thought merely camouflages a child's exultant glee in the recapture of the object, that is, in reencountering it. In our adult propriety, we would not cry out, "Banana!" or "It's the *Acropolis*!" We might instead, according to this line of thinking, demurely tip our hat and say that the thing exists after all, deferring in perhaps a different way to our inner child.

This prospect is undermined by the circumstance that adults are capable of the more childish jubilation. "It's a *wren!*" you cry, when, an occasional birdwatcher, you spy a wren in your feeder, even though you know the species appears with some regularity in your locality. In the exclamation you exult in what I have called reencounter. You establish that you know this bird, and you are excited to see a real specimen. But now suppose a moment later you reflect, "They really *do* exist." If you do so absent any previous doubt as to whether wrens exist, the moment is distinct from the first, and you are having an experience of Freud's thought. It is an experience that, although childlike, children seem not to share.

The experience of the thought appears to resemble the adult experience of the comic and the uncanny, in the way these emerge in Freud's analysis, insofar as it draws upon a piece of childish mental life and adds something to it from later development. Like the comic and the uncanny, the thought is obscure under external scrutiny, and its experiencer cannot say where it comes from. The adult version of it is accompanied by a special feeling, which in his analysis of his experience Freud captured with the idea of a derealization. Like an impromptu joke, the thought appears to irrupt unpremeditated, preceded by an "absence" during which ongoing thought seems to cease.

In a way it resembles a joke more superficially. We cannot mean it seriously. We are saying something a child might say. We aren't joking, however. We mean what we say. We feel something, and the thought arises from what we feel.

Observing this array of properties, Freud might suspect the intervention of unconscious processing, the plunging into the unconscious of preconscious thought, to which he attributes people's spontaneous production of a joke. Indeed, given the elusiveness of the antecedent of Freud's thought—the premise that licenses our surprised affirmation that the object exists—the thought would seem to accord well with the idea of "unconscious revision" Freud cites in the case of joking.

It is difficult to imagine, however, the impetus, and the aim, of a plunge into the unconscious in this case. We wondered earlier at the general, as well as specific, applicability to the thought of the Oedipal strivings Freud ascribes to his case. We then found the more mundane delight in reencounter to which we subsequently ascribed the thought sufficiently compatible with adult mentation that we could see no warrant for the disguise of the delight.

Freud's account of the uncanny might offer a better prototype for the backdrop of the thought, given parallels that appear to exist between that account and the way we have unpacked the thought so far. In Freud's account of the uncanny, the conduit to the experience is no longer a matter of allowing in disguise a form of pleasure to which we no longer think we are entitled. It is a matter of reviving momentarily an outlook we believe we had long since surmounted. So, one *can* kill a person by the mere wish, after all, the animistic premise runs, though one's adult mind rejects the idea as impossible.

Freud himself seems to envision a juxtaposition of this kind as having occurred in his case of the thought. On the one hand, he says, he found himself startled that the Acropolis really exists, and, on the other, he had no idea the existence of the Acropolis was ever in doubt. "So the sea-serpent really *does* exist, that we never believed in," he paraphrases the part of himself surprised at the real existence of the Acropolis as saying. The other part was astonished also, but by something different, namely, the reaction of the first.

The parallel between the uncanny and the thought ends there, however. Magical connections, the basis of the uncanny feeling noted in the preceding example, really don't exist, according to our adult way of thinking. The Acropolis really does exist.

Thus, were the thought to follow the template Freud gives for the uncanny, one would need to experience the Acropolis in the moment as though its existence were as improbable as that of, say, a direct connection between one's thoughts and a remote happening in the world, that is, magic. One would view it not simply as the delightful byproduct of a reencounter but as the outcome of a sleight of hand such that, to one's adult way of thinking, it had no business existing.

The thought could be seen to address a possibility of this kind, if not of a magical connection, then at least of a solipsistic one. The thought feels as though it addresses one's previously held uncertainty about the object's real existence. Contained within that uncertainty could be the impression that the object existed only in one's mind. *I* made this. It was attached to *me*.

The tendency to view the behavior of the world as somehow connected to one, conceived by Freud as part of narcissism and by others (e.g., Piaget, 1923/1959) as egocentrism, is not as alien to routine adult experience as one might think, as formal research documents (e.g., Gilovich, Medvec, and Savitsky, 2000). Here is a personal anecdote:

For a few years running, the principal of my children's school incorporated in his introductory talk to parents on Back-to-School Night the same arresting list of the number of years the average American devotes to different tasks over a normal lifespan. For example, that person spends seven years in the bathroom, six years eating, five years waiting in line, four years cleaning house . . . and, to his point, only three-tenths of 1 percent of their lives in elementary school. I felt stunned and amused the first time I heard the list and remembered it long afterward. When the principal enumerated the same list the following year, I thought something along the lines, "Oh, he's doing it again." I enjoyed it once again, though not with the enchantment of the first time. Over the ensuing couple of years, the impression formed in my mind that the principal was unveilng this great revelation for the first time when I first heard it; then, wisely, he repeated it for succeeding generations of parents new to the school.[3]

One day I became aware that I had formed this impression and recognized in the same moment that, of course, it was only I who was encountering the disquisition for the first time when I first heard it, and the principal had probably delivered it some number of times previously. At the very least, I had no way of knowing when he began to deliver it.

Even if we somehow managed to conceive the object of Freud's thought as locked to our purview, and the feeling figured in Freud's thought, however, the thought denies the archaic premise that purportedly underlies it—"this is attached to me." The experience of the uncanny, on Freud's analysis, by contrast, affirms *its* archaic premise, that self-efficacy at a distance really does operate.

Nonetheless, the thought's archaic premise—the impression that the object existed only in our minds—is created on the spot, though one experiences it as a former impression. It is only when we come upon the supposed new evidence of the object's existence that we become beset by the impression that our previous belief in the reality of the object was tenuous.

Thus, the same observation, which exposes the viewer to the object from a new point of view, simultaneously redraws the earlier experience of the object as unidimensional and supplies the new, independent evidence of the object's existence.

We have come full circle to the point of departure of Freud's essay "A *Disturbance of Memory* on the Acropolis" (my emphasis). It is this ingredient of the experience that calls for an explanation, the memory of not having believed fully in the object's existence, when in fact one believed in it. Natural though this experience, and the resulting confirming thought that the object "really does exist," might appear to be in its context, we remain unable to model it fully. It verges on other ordinary, though ultimately complicated, experiences Freud wrote about—such as the uncanny, the oceanic feeling, the capacity to become absorbed by a story—but it remains distinct. Like these other experiences, it engages a play of emotion; it is not simply a cognitive trick our minds play. We become for the moment awash in a special feeling, which Freud captured at least descriptively with his idea of a derealization. The source and ultimate substance of the feeling, too, remain wrapped in obscurity, though with no less interest on that account.

NOTES

1. I thank the following individuals for their contribution of the anecdotes reported in this chapter, noted more fully in Sugarman (1998): Rüdiger Bittner, Peter Gollwitzer, Eric Santner, and Irene Vogel.

2. For apposite observations, see, for example, Bower (1982) and references cited there, Piaget (1936/1952, 1937/1954), and Watson (1973). On repetition as a fundamental current of psychological life, consider Freud (1940/1989, 17): "The state . . . which an organism has reached gives rise to the tendency to reestablish that state as soon as it is abandoned." Or consider Piaget (1936/1952, 43): "The individual, on however high a level of behavior, tries to reproduce every experience he has lived." Regarding children specifically: "Children will never tire of asking an adult to repeat a game . . . till he is too exhausted to go on. And if a child has been told a nice story, he will insist on hearing it over and over again rather than a new one" (Freud, 1920/1989, 42).

3. I thank Robert Ginsberg for permission to cite his remarks, drawn from George Will (1990, 386–87).

Chapter Ten

What Makes Choice Difficult When It Is: A Freud-Inspired Excursion

Having seen how one can extend Freud's analytic tools beyond his own investigations, we are poised to apply the same methods to a fresh problem. I have selected for this purpose the question of why people with no evident pathology find choice difficult when they do.

The only reference of Freud's to choice in everyday life that I know of appears in his *Psychopathology of Everyday Life* (1901/1989), which he concludes with a chapter on determinism in psychical life and with which we were concerned in chapter 3 of this book. There he discusses the illusion of free will in ordinary people, which comes to a head in matters of choice. Although people have the conviction they have free will, he says, what we call free will does not appear to manifest itself in large decisions. These seem rather to be driven by a compulsion, the feeling that we cannot do other than as we do. Thus, he infers, must the source of the decision come from the promptings of the unconscious. It is with respect to small decisions, with which this chapter will concern itself, that people have the clearest sense they could have acted otherwise and thus that in doing as they did, they acted of their own—free—will. Even these decisions, Freud says, receive input from the unconscious, such that our hand is turned, sometimes more and sometimes less, by promptings of which we are not aware (p. 324).

That the unconscious may contribute to the direction in which our selection process ultimately swings, or for that matter to how long we suspend ourselves in indecision, does not help us gain purchase on the subtext that sustains the deliberative process, our concern here. The impression of freedom does figure in that picture, and we shall begin with that impression.

A thirteen-year-old acquaintance out to dinner with a group of people including her mother rejected a teabag she had ordered so she might choose from "the box," which she had observed a patron perusing at another table. The box was a wooden case containing the restaurant's numerous herbal tea offerings. The girl wanted to choose from the box so she could make her selection from all the choices. But when the box arrived, she asked her mother to pick first.

Many people have experienced versions of this scene, especially in Western industrial cultures in which choices abound. One is drawn to the restaurant with plentiful choices, only to long and even ask for external support to make up one's mind about what to have. One hopes for admission to several colleges only to despair over which one to attend. In line with these observations, formal research has shown that consumers are more likely to make purchases or other choices when they have fewer, rather than more, options (Iyengar and Lepper, 2000; Schwartz, 2004; Tversky and Shafir, 1992).

Why do people find choice difficult when they do? I limit the discussion in this chapter to everyday choices of a mainly agreeable nature. The answers seem straightforward. When we find ourselves faced with numerous options roughly equal in their appeal, we cannot easily determine the best one (Simon, 1982). Insofar as we fancy more than one option and yet must choose only one, we must give something up and do this only with great difficulty. It has been generally accepted at least since Freud (e.g., 1913/1989), that when we lose something or someone, or are threatened with the loss, we attach increased value to the thing or person. Hence our difficulty in relinquishing even inconsequential objects, for instance, the aging shirt we finally agree to discard, the pen we earned by serving as a participant in university research when we are offered a mug in exchange for it (Brehm, 1966; Kahneman, Knetsch, and Thaler, 1990). Or we fear later regret (Bell, 1982). We fall prey to regret most easily the more accessible we perceive an alternative course of action to have been (Miller and Taylor, 1995). Consciously made choices make alternatives highly salient. I could have had this stereo rather than that one merely by *choice*.

Training a critical lens on these factors, as Freud did upon the first wave of explanations of his experience on the Acropolis, however, one discovers that although they may operate, the factors themselves call for explanation.

It is not obvious why something, such as a selection of dishes on a menu, has to be better than are the others or why we have to have the "best," even if we can identify a best. "What's wrong with number two?" shouted Morrie Schwartz, late Brandeis professor and irrepressible subject of Mitch Albom's *Tuesdays with Morrie* (1997), after Brandeis had pulled ahead at a basketball game, prompting the students to chant, "We're number one! We're number one!" (p. 159).

Insofar as we fear later regret or the sense of loss associated with it, the question arises of why we feel loss and regret so easily and dread them so much. What does it matter if the penne and eggplant might have tasted better than the vegetable quiche, or as good but different? Let us try to reason through the possibilities a little further.

Perhaps we try to identify the best to attain the adequate or the good. We cannot tell from a menu how different selections will look or taste. We may lack a clear sense of the kind of taste we are in the mood for or may feel conflicted between a tasty dish and one we consider healthier. Insofar as we aim for the best, we increase the likelihood we will avoid disappointment.

This scenario raises the problem I have already described. It remains unclear, especially when we are attempting to choose among agreeable options, why the sense of potential disappointment looms as large as it does or why, to the extent we go on to experience the disappointment (e.g., Connolly and

Zeelenberg, 2002), we are so prone to it. So what if I end up feeling I might have preferred the penne and eggplant after I ordered the quiche?

Further thought raises questions, moreover, about the supposed worries that drive this indecision. It is when the penne and eggplant and the vegetable quiche are offered together that I suddenly worry about balancing healthfulness against taste or wonder what type of dish I'm "really" in the mood for. Before I enter the restaurant, or if I am offered either dish alone in a field of less agreeable options, I am less likely to raise these concerns. (These effects, observable in common experience, may be extrapolated from existing research on people's "reason-based" choice-making; see, e.g., Shafir, Simonson, and Tversky, 1993.)

Perhaps we are conditioned to seek the best: the best quality, the best value, or the selection that suits us the best. For example, although I may find several brands of facial tissue both acceptable and affordable, merely through force of habit I strive to identify the best quality, best value, or best in some other respect among the group.

Even if force of habit mediates this effort, the tenacity of the habit, the fierceness with which we try to meet its demands, and the anxiety and regret we feel when we think we have failed at our task require explanation. I could stop or alter many other habits I have learned, for example, brushing my teeth after every meal, reading the newspaper at breakfast, watering my plants on Saturday. Most people would find it difficult to give up or even consider giving up the search for the best on occasions when, faced with more than one attractive option, they persist in the search. At the same time, they would probably find themselves hard pressed to articulate fully why they need the best.

Economic theory has traditionally assumed that people normally attempt to "maximize their utilities," to strive for the best, for instance, in the sense of the best value for the money or the best quality regardless of the money. Sometimes when the cost of determining the best becomes sufficiently high, when, for example, one cannot easily determine the full range of one's options or their exact value, one "satisfices" instead. One strives for a selection that is satisfactory rather than optimal, having optimized instead the expenditure on one's time, energy, and other resources (March, 1978; Simon, 1982). Having decided she will never be able to determine the best house on the market for her needs, for example, a buyer might scan the prospects for a house she finds acceptable on the dimensions that matter to her.

Discussions of these strategies leave unanswered the question of why we search for the best on the occasions when we do, or why we satisfice when we do. It remains obscure why, when we have narrowed our menu selection to a few dishes we cannot easily rank-order, we continue to belabor the task of identifying which is the best, rather than choosing arbitrarily or whimsically. It remains obscure why we cannot settle for the good or even the wonderful and why instead we anticipate and sometimes experience a sense of error and loss.

Given the apparent inaccessibility of the recalcitrance of choice to face-value explanation, we might turn to one discussion of Freud's that touches upon indecision, albeit in the context of pathology. Freud's "Rat Man" case history (1909a/1963) deals with a young lieutenant suffering from obsessive-compulsive disorder, whose disease manifested, among other ways, in excruciating indecision over both large and small matters. Freud ascribes the symptom to the profound ambivalences that pervaded the man's unconscious, including buried conflicts with his now-dead father and related ambivalences concerning the woman he wanted to marry. In this and other cases, Freud detected in the poles of the seemingly inconsequential decisions over which patients struggled a positive thrust and a negative, hostile one.

Thus, on one occasion the lieutenant felt compelled to leap from his carriage to move a stone in the road along which his lady friend was to drive some time later. He then decided he ought not to move the stone and replaced it in its original position, so her carriage might falter over it (1909a/1963, 50).

Another obsessional patient flung from a park path a branch he thought might injure people, only to return under a compulsion afterward to move it back to its original position. He feared it might injure someone in its new location, where it protruded from a hedge. Anyone but the patient, Freud reports, would have seen that the first location of the branch, the place in the path, had a greater potential for injury than did the second (1909a/1963, 51).

In both cases, a first, philanthropic impulse was undone by a second, contrary one, despite the philanthropic-sounding cover story in the second case. Thus, according to Freud's more extended analyses, could each case have represented the enactment of the patients' unresolved feelings of love and hatred.

The grounds for Freud's attributions aside, note the explanatory work this account does. An unresolved conflict, especially one of which the person is incompletely aware, continues to struggle for expression, so both poles receive their due. Were grounds to exist for the attribution, it would close gaps left open by other explanatory efforts. We would know why someone might do and undo a decision, which, over repeated cycles, is what indecision entails, despite the evident cost to the person in convenience and comfort.

Just as we questioned the wider applicability of the unconscious motives Freud ascribes to his thought on the Acropolis, we do not know whether all cases of indecision, including all cases of protracted and even pathological indecision, emerge from a base of displaced ambivalence. Granted that even ordinary indecision boasts more pathos than does "Freud's thought," we may gain further purchase on it instead by again deploying Freud's broader tactic of exploring the possible contribution of our developmental history to our problem.

Babies do not choose so much as pick what is salient or accept what is good, in the sense in which a scout bee explores potential blossoms until it finds a good flower with no cognizance of, and hence no concern about, the options it may be foregoing. Thus, babies play with a given toy, or not, or take a proffered morsel to eat, or not (as is suggested by trends in children's play; e.g., McCune, 1995; Sugarman, 1981). They do not wonder whether to try this toy *or* that and thus experience none of the distress that potentially attends choice. They do not concern themselves with which option is best or whether they may feel regret. They do not compare.

To choose or to understand the idea of a choice, one must conceive alternatives. "There are As, and there are Bs. I like A. I like B. Shall I have A *or* B?" By two-and-a-half, at least at times, children appear to pause, consider, and choose in this way in the course of their activity. In a study of free play I conducted with colleagues, for instance, a two-and-a-half-year-old girl walked to the sandbox in our playroom and put her hands on her hips as she surveyed the objects lying near the sandbox. She picked up a small wooden saucer, put it down, picked up a pot and scrutinized its bottom, put down the pot, picked up and turned over the wooden saucer, and then walked with the saucer across the room (Sugarman, 2005, and references cited there). The behavior is consistent with children's development by two-and-a-half of the ability to combine two foci of organization in a variety of laboratory tasks (Sugarman, 1982; also DeLoache, 1987; Greenfield, Nelson, and Saltzman, 1972).

Before this development occurs, children's behavior reflects the contrast just noted also when, instead of playing on their own, they are prodded by someone else to choose—for instance, the ball *or* the car. Neither the query nor the circumstance appears to register with them. In two studies in which children at yearly intervals between one-and-a-half and four-and-a-half were given a choice of two objects to play with, children of one-and-a-half often reached for both things (Sugarman, 2005). As noted by observers of infants, when babies see things, they reach for them (e.g., Piaget, 1936/1952; Sully, 1895/2000).

To choose, therefore, is not natural for us and may remain unnatural even once we develop the capacity to conceive and consider alternatives. We do not naturally deprive ourselves of things we want. When asked to choose between two toys for a gift to take home, for example, a child of two-and-a-half in one of our studies deliberated, procrastinated (for instance, by playing with the objects), and changed her mind after making her selection.

One theory of why we adults have difficulty with choice, then, is that we "reach for both things" and do not easily give up what we want.

Nonetheless, the model of the lunging baby does not entirely capture what we feel when we agonize over a choice. The lunging baby reflexively grasps what is desired and resists letting go. When we have narrowed a choice to, say, two shirts to wear or two movies to go see, we do not want both. We do not know which one we want.

Not to know which thing we want presupposes an awareness of a choice and hence of an inevitable loss. We realize we may have A *or* B and know that selecting one of them will necessitate our giving up the other. Parents who contributed entries to a study of child "choice diaries" I conducted reported spontaneously a concern on the part of their (older) children with loss.

The mother of a five-year-old wrote, for instance, that her son had difficulty making especially the sorts of the decisions that excluded one thing over another and that finally making the choice minimized the boy's pleasure in the thing gained, though it also seemed to offer relief. She observed him become paralyzed with indecision in choosing between different colored Popsicles, for example (Sugarman, 2005, 18–19).

More was occurring in the events the writer describes than that someone was taking away what the child wanted, against the child's protests. The boy understood that when he chose, one Popsicle would be kept and the others relinquished. He felt loath to give up the others, though he knew he had to do so. Indeed, on a different occasion, afraid the motor boat in which he had joined his father for a trip to secure more fuel would run out of the fuel it had, the same child pleaded to be returned to the family's houseboat. Once safely returned, and his father having departed again for the fuel, the boy was sorry he had returned and asked again to join his father.

But something still more than a sense of loss and the resistance to it seems to intrude into adult choice. We want the best, or the better, and fear making the *wrong* choice. When after torturous deliberation I finally decide to buy a lightweight cotton sunhat with black under its rim and another color on top, rather than a firmer but slightly heavier canvas hat that is all one color, I do not despair that I must leave one hat behind. I wonder whether I picked the better one, or, alternatively, whether I made a mistake.

One wants to know what we mean by *best* in situations of this kind. Most straightforward would be the appropriateness of means to a given end, for instance, the appropriateness of a sunhat to shielding one from the sun. Indicative of this type of concern, after sweeping sand with a duster from some saucers onto a table, as she "washed" the dishes, and then brushing the sand to the edge of the table, one three-and-a-half-year-old girl searched our laboratory playroom until she found a basin into which she could sweep the sand (Sugarman, 2005, 19–20).

In the example I have given about the sunhats, however, my problem is not that of calculating the appropriate means to an end. The problem is the determination of my preference: Do I want a lighter hat with mixed colors or a hat of uniform color, at some sacrifice to the lightness? For the narrow purpose at hand, namely, procuring a hat I like that will shield me from the sun, either hat would serve.

Therefore, although my locutions, of wanting to determine the better hat and of fearing a mistake, might differ from those of the little boy who could not decide among Popsicles for fear of what he would have to give up, my underlying dilemma might resemble his. I like the lighter weight hat for its lightness and the likelihood it would consequently trap less heat than would the canvas hat. I like the canvas hat for its ability to hold its shape and not wrinkle, and I prefer its uniform color. Would that I could have all the things I like: a lighter, softer fabric, the ability to hold shape and not wrinkle, and a single color. But I cannot.

Actually, I could. I could buy both hats.

Although this strategy might work on some occasions, it would not work for all. We have logistical constraints—for instance, our closet can hold only so much, or our finances may limit us—that would keep us on track to procure one thing, or we might simply want only one. We have desires, in other words, that would ultimately compete with the satisfaction we might otherwise achieve from rejecting the choice and taking everything. We do not "reach for both things"; we want to choose.

Perhaps when, for one reason or another, I can't or won't have everything I want, I *compromise* for the best or, in the case of the hats, the better. The best selection may give us as much of what we want as we can possibly get, because we choose the qualities we want or value the most. Additionally, insofar as one selection is better than all the rest, then we lose the least in rejecting the rest. The difficulty arises here that we may have trouble deciding which qualities we want or value the most. Thus we will not easily determine the best (or better) selection and continue doggedly to search for it. Even though we do not know which it is, we appear unable to bear the prospect of not attaining it.

We seem to manage comparable losses when they arise outside our control. Imagine that as I deliberate between the two sunhats, I learn one of them is unavailable. It is reserved for another customer. It would seem easier to give up something in this situation, not only because one has been asked to do so, but because it is easier to relinquish it when one cannot have it than when one could have it.

Thus, we have difficulty losing by our own hand. But this is the essence of choice: freedom from external constraint in what we do and thus the assumption of full responsibility for the consequences that transpire. In a case of completely free choice we do not fall back even on the notion that others might enjoin one or more of our alternatives. Any choice is possible. The result can be paralyzing, as we have seen. With no guiding hand such as a god, wrote Sartre (1946/1965, 41), we drown in a sea of possibility, despairing because we have nothing either within or outside us to cling to (see also Dworkin, 1982; Fromm, 1941; Kierkegaard, 1849/1980; Schwartz, 2004). Consequently we intrude others into our choices, as did the girl who requested the tea box so she could see all the choices and then asked her mother to choose first.

The sense of personal responsibility seems implicit already in the little boy's uncertainty about which Popsicle he wanted and the fear his mother thinks he experienced of his impending loss. Unlike lunging babies who reach for what they want and resist external efforts to have things taken away, the boy knew *he* would give something up. Which thing it would be, moreover, was up to him.

That personal responsibility, and not only loss, lies behind people's agitation over choice is suggested by the ineffectiveness of another potential antidote to the agitation. When we suffer a loss we could not avoid we may find our pain eased insofar as we mourn what we have lost and allow ourselves slowly to release it, as we do when we have lost a cherished person, pet, or object (Freud, 1917b/1984). Such advice offers little consolation in a spasm of indecision. We are raging against the self for potential error rather than despairing at a fate external forces may impose.

The sense of regret and fear of error to which we fall prey after infancy make the recognition of personal responsibility explicit. These sensibilities build upon the capacity, which develops, to remember the past and anticipate the future. To regret an action one needs to understand one had a choice and to recognize and remember alternative paths one might have taken. To fear error one needs to concern oneself with the aftermath of an action not yet taken. Toddlers may remain largely free of experiences of this kind insofar as they live more in the here and now than adults do. Rather than fall prey to lingering memories of options they abandoned, they become distracted by new input.

One last antidote to our quandaries in choice might be to emulate this model. We could choose more or less as babies do, selecting an alternative that suited and quickly becoming indifferent to options we left behind, regardless of whether we had noticed them. But in this way, although we might spare ourselves the pain of indecision, we would not know much about the world. We come to know it by investing in it, to borrow one of Freud's terms for our expenditure of psychical energy. We invest in it, according to Freud, even in the mere act of attention and in the formation of interest all the more so (1911/1963). Consciously deliberated choice goes beyond these minimal expenditures to the awaking of desire and the exploratory visualization of the consummation of the desire. Any such deployment of energy establishes a libido position, as Freud calls it, and, as we shall examine more fully next, we give up our libido positions only reluctantly.

Chapter Eleven

Mourning and Mental Health: "On Transience" (1916), "Mourning and Melancholia" (1917)

Thus far we have followed Freud in pursuing anomalies he identified in mental life and extracting an anomaly of our own for study. In each case where Freud identified the anomaly—the "oceanic feeling," the captivation of pleasure reading, jokes and the comic, the uncanny, and his experience on the Acropolis—it seemed possible, at least after some work, to discern the anomaly he perceived. The puzzle Freud identifies in the passage from his paper "On Transience" (1916/1985) with which I opened the book remains opaque.

The pain of mourning strikes the ordinary observer as self-evident. One loves; one loses one's love; one suffers. Freud himself declared that we give up "libido positions" only with great difficulty; hence, for instance, our liability to fantasize (1908/1985). But in two celebrated essays (1916/1985, 1917b/1984), he lamented that, even granting the understandable opposition of the ego to the relinquishing of its (love) objects, he could not account for the extraordinary pain the loss of our objects brings.

Ten years later, in an appendix to his *Inhibitions, Symptoms, and Anxiety* (1926/1989), he claimed to have found the missing explanation. Upon reading the comment, one appreciates, perhaps for the first time, the narrowly technical question Freud was raising earlier in what one could easily perceive as a more far-reaching admission of failure. It was within his "economic" theory, as he had said earlier, that he could not account for the pain of mourning. What he meant by this, according to the later comment, was that he could not extrapolate to the source of the vast mass of energy consumed by grief. He perceived that energy greatly to exceed the pool of energy people consume in even an intense love for the object during its lifetime. This circumstance leaves the question of where the apparent excess comes from.

Limited though it is, Freud's reply opens up another intriguing line of inquiry into ordinary mental life, this time regarding the nature of mental health itself. I therefore conclude with brief reflections on his remarks.

When one mourns, Freud says in repeating his earlier assessment, reality-testing tells one the object no longer exists, and one must face the task of detaching one's libido from it. The act of separation proves painful, he now adds, because the object, still the recipient of a "high degree of cathexis [viz., psychical energy]" (Freud, 1926/1989, 109), can no longer satisfy the cathexis, and the unsatisfied cathexis builds. The accumulation of unsatisfied cathexis produces the pain the mourner feels.

The mechanism at work in this effect operates more transparently, Freud suggests, in the frantic cries of babies whose mother has vanished, in consequence of which the babies' needs and their longing for the mother mount exponentially. The mother reappears, however, and the accumulating cathexis dissipates, able to find other uses. Over time, babies come to expect the mother to reappear after she disappears. Thus, in time, the build-up of cathexis during her absence lessens. When we lose an object permanently, no such reprieve occurs, and the pain becomes excruciating.

The onslaught of cathexis embodied by mourning mimics the economic conditions produced by physical pain, according to the new account. In the experience of physical pain, a stimulus impinging from the inner or outer periphery of the body breaches the organism's protective devices and unleashes a flood of energy from which there is no escape. One cannot escape the onslaught because it is internal (Freud, 1920/1989). Consequently, we experience pain.

With this elaboration of his theory, Freud was able to account for the tremendous energy consumed by mourning, in a system that has finite energy. The lost object arouses the cathexis it elicited formerly, only now the cathexis remains unsatisfied, consequently accrues, and thus produces extreme pain.

Insofar as Freud felt perplexed initially by a purely quantitative puzzle, he seems to have addressed his concern with this addendum. His pairing of mourning with the suffering of physical pain suggests further amplification of mourning, however.

Mourning and the pain from physical insult share two features, beside the energic dynamic Freud describes, that distinguish the two conditions from other varieties of painful experience.

First, the recovery from mourning and physical pain follows a different course from that followed by other forms of pain, even within the category of pain generated from within. As Freud notes, whereas one can flee from pain caused by an external stimulus, such as a hot stove, the escape from endogenously generated pain requires a more complicated solution. Some pain in this category can be relieved by action on the part of the afflicted person. For instance, although one cannot flee from the pain produced by an instinctual need, such as hunger, one may satisfy the need. One can do this by bringing about an alteration in the external world, for example, by crying to obtain the provider of food or procuring the food oneself (Freud, 1915a/1984). One cannot relieve the pain of either physical injury or mourning by any comparable intervention. The pain in these cases dissipates only through healing, a gradual process one can influence only peripherally.

Second, both pain from physical injury and mourning draw sufferers' attention away from the ego. In the case of physical pain, one's attention is drawn to the site of the breach. One thinks of little beyond the throbbing pain of a broken limb or the discomfort of an acute ailment, for example. In mourning, one becomes consumed by the object and its loss, as Freud (1917b/1984) notes. In either case, one may become absorbed in one's pain or turn from the external world; neither of these dispositions necessarily implies a preoccupation with the self in itself.

Either form of suffering may be hijacked by other processes. Hypochondria may usurp normal pain mechanisms, for example, and melancholia (depression) converges with mourning in numerous important respects, as Freud (1917b/1984, 252) details.

These mixed cases lack the two features I identified that distinguish nonpathological mourning and the experience of physical pain from other painful conditions: recovery through spontaneous healing and the setting aside of the self. Instances of pathology, they require intervention for recovery, and they emanate from a self absorbed in itself.

It follows from this contrast that the experience of physical pain and mourning, and the recovery from them, signify mental health. They are distinguished by spontaneous remission and a lack of self-preoccupation, whereas pathology is defined by the opposite of these features.

At the same time, both the endurance of physical pain and mourning and recovery from them are passive processes. We do not feel our pain or disregard the self through any act of will. Thus we do not, in turning from self in these experiences, exhibit any particular virtuousness, as we might do when we intentionally set the self aside on someone else's behalf, in an act of self-sacrifice, for instance. Our passivity in both cases also distinguishes them from other forms of reality-function in which we act deliberately to effect changes that will enable us to reach our goals. "Energetic and successful" people, Freud writes, "succeed by [their] efforts in turning [their] wishful fantasies into reality" (1909b/1989, 55). Mourning and the endurance of physical pain entail no effort, other than the restraint from any sort of intervention that might disrupt them or the process of healing from them.

In this elaboration of Freud's conception, one may discern a template for the realms of ordinary experience addressed by Freud and covered in this book, as well as the sanguinity they connote. One's immersion in a book, indulgence in the comical, and ability to reach the epiphany that something really exists despite the obviousness of the claim all presuppose a setting aside of self and a relinquishing of any other sort of control over the unfolding of the experience. One could add the uncanny as an aesthetic experience to this list, though it can be inspired by pathological dispositions, as the Rat Man case shows. Indeed, efforts in either of these directions—the intrusion of the self or the guidance of the process—will undermine and effectively terminate the experiences.

It is perhaps this sort of egoless and effortless effect Freud had in mind when he said of some of the processes, jokes in particular, that they involved a plunging of ongoing thought into the unconscious. Normally, in Freud's writings, which dwell upon psychopathology, the plunge into the unconscious is taken in the ego's defense. In these cases it is the opposite. It is the ego at play, we might say at integration, an integration that, paradoxically, entails the ego's temporary annihilation.

In this plunge, as Freud calls it, these processes tap a fragment of the mental life of our childhoods, which, however, they also complicate. We see in them the delicate interplay of child and adult in the adult mind. It is more than an interplay. It is a synergy, rich in texture and detail, that Freud had the audacity and the insight to expose and describe.

References

Albom, M. 1997. *Tuesdays with Morrie: An old man, a young man, and life's greatest lesson.* New York: Doubleday.

Aristotle. 1941. *The basic works of Aristotle.* Ed. R. McKeon. New York: Random House.

Bell, D. E. 1982. Regret in decision-making under uncertainty. *Operations Research* 30, 961–81.

Bower, T. G. R. 1982. *Development in infancy.* 2nd ed. San Francisco: Freeman.

Brehm, J. W. 1966. *A theory of psychological reactance.* New York: Academic Press.

Brown, R. 1973. *A first language: The early stages.* Cambridge, MA: Harvard.

Cole, M., and E. Subbotsky. 1991. The fate of stages past: Reflections on the heterogeneity of thinking from the perspective of cultural-historical psychology. Paper presented at the symposium "The Cultural Environment in Psychology" honoring Ernst Boesch, Merlingen, Switzerland, October 21–24.

Connolly, T., and M. Zeelenberg. 2002. Regret in decision making. *Current Directions in Psychological Science* 11, 212–16.

DeLoache, J. S. 1987. Rapid change in the symbolic functioning of very young children. *Science* 238, 1556–57.

Dworkin, G. 1982. Is more choice better than less? *Midwest Studies in Philosophy* 7, 47–61.

Fechner, G. T. 1897. *Vorschule der Äesthetik.* 2 vols. 2nd ed. Leipzig. Cited in Freud, 1905/1989, 165.

Fodor, J. A. 1972. Some reflections on L. S. Vygotsky's *Thought and language*. *Cognition* 1, 85–93.

Freud, S. 1900/1965. *The interpretation of dreams*. Trans. J. Strachey. New York: Avon.

——. 1901/1989. *The psychopathology of everyday life*. Trans. J. Strachey. New York: Norton.

——. 1905/1989. *Jokes and their relation to the unconscious*. Trans. J. Strachey. New York: Norton.

——. 1906/1985. Psychopathic characters on the stage. In *The Pelican Freud Library* 14, ed. A. Dickson, trans. J. Strachey, pp. 119–28. Harmondsworth, UK: Penguin.

——. 1908/1985. Creative writers and daydreaming. In *The Pelican Freud Library* 14, ed. A. Dickson, trans. J. Strachey, pp. 129–42. Harmondsworth, UK: Penguin.

——. 1909a/1963. Notes upon a case of obsessional neurosis. In *Freud: Three case histories*, ed. P. Reiff, translation supervised by J. Riviere, pp. 15–102. New York: Collier-Macmillan.

——. 1909b/1989. *Five lectures on psychoanalysis*. Trans. J. Strachey. New York: Norton.

——. 1911/1963. Formulations regarding two principles in mental functioning. In *Freud: General psychological theory*, ed. P. Reiff, translation supervised by J. Riviere, pp. 21–28. New York: Collier-Macmillan.

——. 1913/1989. *Totem and taboo*. Trans. J. Strachey. New York: Norton.

——. 1915a/1984. Instincts and their vicissitudes. In *The Pelican Freud Library* 11, ed. A. Richards, trans. J. Strachey, pp. 105–38. Harmondsworth, UK: Penguin.

——. 1915b/1984. The unconscious. In *The Pelican Freud Library* 11, ed. A. Richards, trans. J. Strachey, pp. 159–222. Harmondsworth, UK: Penguin.

——. 1916/1985. On transience. In *The Pelican Freud Library* 14, ed. A. Dickson, trans. J. Strachey, pp. 283–90. Harmondsworth, UK: Penguin.

——. 1917a/1984. A metapsychological supplement to the theory of dreams. In *The Pelican Freud Library* 11, ed. A. Richards, trans. J. Strachey, pp. 223–44. Harmondsworth, UK: Penguin.

——. 1917b/1984. Mourning and melancholia. In *The Pelican Freud Library* 11, ed. A. Richards, trans. J. Strachey, pp. 245–68. Harmondsworth, UK: Penguin.

——. 1917c/1989. *Introductory lectures on psychoanalysis*. Trans. J. Strachey. New York: Norton.

——. 1919/1985. The "Uncanny," In *The Pelican Freud Library* 14, ed. A. Dickson, trans. J. Strachey, pp. 335–76. Harmondsworth, UK: Penguin.

——. 1920/1989. *Beyond the pleasure principle*. Trans. J Strachey. New York: Norton.

——. 1924/1963. The economic problem in masochism. In *Freud: General psychological theory*, ed. P. Reiff, translation supervised by J. Riviere, pp. 190–201. New York: Collier-Macmillan.

——. 1926/1989. *Inhibitions, symptoms, and anxiety*. New York: Norton.

——. 1927a/1985. On humour. In *The Pelican Freud Library* 14, ed. A. Dickson, trans. J. Strachey, pp. 425–34. Harmondsworth, UK: Penguin.

——. 1927b/1989. *The future of an illusion*. Trans. J. Strachey. New York: Norton.

——. 1930/1989. *Civilization and its discontents*. Trans. J. Strachey. New York: Norton.

——. 1936a/1950. Brief an Romain Rolland: Eine Erinnerungsstörung auf der Akropolis. *Gesammelte Werke*, 16. London: Imago.

——. 1936b/1984. A disturbance of memory on the Acropolis: An open letter to Romain Rolland on the occasion of his seventieth birthday. In *The Pelican Freud Library* 11, ed. A. Richards, trans. J. Strachey, pp. 443–56. Harmondsworth, UK: Penguin.

——. 1940/1989. *An outline of psychoanalysis*. New York: Norton.

Fromm, E. 1941. *Escape from freedom*. New York: Avon.

Gilovich, T., V. H. Medvec, and K. Savitsky. 2000. The spotlight effect in social judgment: An egocentric bias in estimations of the salience of one's own actions and appearance. *Journal of Personality and Social Psychology* 78, 211–22.

Greenfield, P. M., K. Nelson, and E. Saltzman. 1972. The development of rule-bound strategies for manipulating seriated cups: A parallel between action and grammar. *Cognitive Psychology* 3, 291–310.

Greeno, J. G., M. S. Riley, and R. Gelman. 1984. Conceptual competence and children's counting. *Cognitive Psychology* 16, 94–143.

Grimm, M., and W. Grimm. 1877. *Deutsches Wörterbuch* 4. Leipzig. Cited in Freud, 1919/1985, 346.

Harris, P. L. 1983. Infant cognition. In *Handbook of child psychology*, ed. P. H. Mussen, vol. 2, *Infancy and developmental psychobiology*, ed. M. M. Haith and J. J. Campos, pp. 689–782. New York: Wiley.

Heymans, G. 1896. Ästhetische Untersuchengen in Anschluss an die Lippssche Theories des Komischen. *Z. Psychol. Physiol. Sinnesorg.* 11, 31 and 333. Cited in Freud, 1905/1989, 185.

Hoffmann, E. T. A. 1952. The sand-man. In *Eight tales of Hoffmann*, trans. J. M. Cohen. London: Pan Books.

Iyengar, S. S., and M. B. Lepper. 2000. When choice is demotivating: Can one desire too much of a good thing? *Journal of Personality and Social Psychology* 79, 995–1006.

Kahneman, D., J. L. Knetsch, and R. H. Thaler. 1990. Experimental tests of the endowment effect and the Coase theorem. *Journal of Political Economy* 98, 1325–48.

Kandel, E. R. 1999. Biology and the future of psychoanalysis: A new intellectual framework for psychiatry revisited. *American Journal of Psychiatry* 156, 505–24.

Kierkegaard, S. 1849/1980. *The sickness unto death: A Christian psychological exposition for upbuilding and awakening*. Trans. H. V. Hong and E. H. Hong. Princeton, NJ: Princeton University Press.

Kleinpaul, E. 1890. *Die Rätsel der Sprache*. Leipzig. Cited in Freud, 1905/1989, 158.

Lear, J. 1998. *Open-minded: Working out the logic of the soul*. Cambridge, MA: Harvard.

Lichtenberg, G. C. von (The Elder). 1853. Witzige und satirische Einfälle, vol. 2 of New Enlarged Edition: Göttingen. Cited in Freud (1905/1989), 97–103.

Lively, P. 1989. *Moon tiger*. New York: HarperCollins.

March, J. G. 1978. Bounded rationality, ambiguity, and the engineering of choice. *Bell Journal of Economics* 9, 587–608.

Matthews, G. B. 1980. *Philosophy and the young child*. Cambridge, MA: Harvard.

McCune, L. 1995. A normative study of representational play at the transition to language. *Developmental Psychology* 31, 198–206.

Miller, D. T., and B. R. Taylor. 1995. Counterfactual thought, regret, and superstition: How to avoid kicking yourself. In *What might have been: The social psychology of counterfactual thinking*, ed. N. Roese and J. M. Olson, pp. 305–31. Mahwah, NJ: Erlbaum.

Piaget, J. 1923/1959. *The language and thought of the child.* Trans. M. Gabain. New York: Meridan.

——. 1936/1952. *The origins of intelligence in children.* Trans. M. Cook. New York: International Universities Press.

——. 1937/1954. *The construction of reality in the child.* Trans. M. Cook. New York: Basic.

Pomorsky, K. Ed. 1987. *Language, poetry, and poetics: The generation of the 1890s: Jakobson, Trubetskoy, Majakovsky.* Proceedings of the first Roman Jakobson colloquium at the Massachusetts Institute of Technology, October 5–6, 1984. Berlin and New York: de Gruyter.

Sartre, J.-P. 1946/1965. The humanism of existentialism. Trans. B. Frechtman. In J.-P. Sartre, *The philosophy of existentialism*, ed. W. Baskin, pp. 31-62. New York: Philosophical Library.

Schwartz, B. 2004. *The paradox of choice: Why more is less.* New York: Ecco.

Shachter, D. L. 2001. *The seven sins of memory: How the mind forgets and remembers.* Boston: Houghton Mifflin.

Shafir, E., I. Simonson, and A. Tversky. 1993. Reason-based choice. *Cognition* 49, 11–36.

Simon, H. A. 1982. *Models of bounded rationality.* Vol. 3, *Empirically grounded economic reason.* Cambridge, MA: MIT.

Strachey, J. 1965. Editor's introduction to S. Freud (1901/1989) *The psychopathology of everyday life.* New York: Norton.

Sugarman, S. 1981. The cognitive basis of classification in very young children: An analysis of object ordering trends. *Child Development* 52, 1172–78.

——. 1982. Developmental change in early representational intelligence: Evidence from spatial classification strategies and related verbal expressions. *Cognitive Psychology* 14, 410–49.

——. 1983. *Children's early thought: Developments in classification.* New York: Cambridge.

——. 1987. *Piaget's construction of the child's reality.* New York: Cambridge.

——. 1998. *Freud on the Acropolis: Reflections on a paradoxical response to the real.* New York: Basic.

——. 2005. Choice and freedom: Reflections and observations based upon human development. *International Journal of Infant Observation* 7, 11–25.

Sully, J. 1895/2000. *Studies of childhood.* London: Free Association Books.

Tversky, A., and E. Shafir. 1992. Choice under conflict: the dynamics of deferred decision. *Psychological Science* 3, 358–61.

Watson, J. S. 1973. Smiling, cooing, and the game. *Merrill-Palmer Quarterly* 18, 323–39.

Will, G. 1990. *Suddenly: The American idea abroad and at home 1986–1990.* New York: Free Press.

Index

About the Author

Susan Sugarman is professor of psychology at Princeton University, where she also teaches in the Council of the Humanities, has published empirical and theoretical works on the cognitive development of children. Attracted by Freud's investigative tactic of using the child to understand the adult, she has written more recently on Freud, including *Freud on the Acropolis: Reflections on a Paradoxical Response to the Real.*

www.ingramcontent.com/pod-product-compliance
Lightning Source LLC
LaVergne TN
LVHW011513200926
848484LV00001B/29